Great Expectations?

By the same author
Just Like Him! (BRF)
Renewal in Worship (Marshalls)
The Gospel Connection (Morehouse Barlow)

The Bible Reading Fellowship was founded 'to encourage the systematic and intelligent reading of the Bible, to emphasize its spiritual message and to take advantage of new light shed on Holy Scripture'.

Over the years the Fellowship has proved a trustworthy guide for those who want an open, informed and contemporary approach to the Bible. It retains a sense of the unique authority of Scripture as a prime means by which God communicates.

As an ecumenical organization, the Fellowship embraces all Christian traditions and its readers are to be found in most parts of the world.

Great Expectations?

Bible training for evangelism in parishes

Michael Marshall

the bible reading fellowship

Dedicated to
Charles Bewick R.I.P.
friend, priest and
witness to Pentecost

The Bible Reading Fellowship
Ground Floor
Warwick House
25 Buckingham Palace Road
London SW1W 0PP

First published 1991

Bible quotations are taken from the New International Version,
copyright 1984 by International Bible Society.

British Library Cataloguing in Publication Data
Marshall, Michael 1936–
    Great expectations? : bible training for evangelism in parishes.
    1. Christian church. Evangelism. Use of Bible
    I. Title II. Bible Reading Fellowship
    269.2

ISBN 0-900164-87-5

Typeset by Barnes Design + Print Group, Maidenhead, England
Printed by J.W. Arrowsmith Ltd., Bristol, England

Contents

Acknowledgements

The author wishes to acknowledge greatly his debt of gratitude to John Stott, in his newly published commentary on the Book of Acts — *The Spirit, The Church and the World* (Intervarsity 1989), and also to William Barclay whose Daily Bible Study Series on Acts have proved a refreshing guide to much that is written in these pages.

The author would also wish to acknowledge with gratitude all who helped him in the writing of this book — not least the many Bible students in different parts of the world who have shared with him in Bible Classes.

Finally, a personal note. Dennis Napier and Michael King have been a source of encouragement throughout the production of this book. Mary Baddeley has typed the manuscript in record time and helped the author with editorial suggestions. Canon Paul Jobson helped to draw up the Vigil Service for Pentecost Eve which comes at the end of the book, setting Bible study within worship and witness.

Preface

This book of Bible studies is offered as a resource to parish Bible study groups to help parishes to prepare for a new commitment to evangelization. It is intended to move us from the celebration of Easter joy to a new commitment to Pentecost mission and to reach a climax on the eve of Pentecost when the whole body of Bible students from a given district will hopefully come together to celebrate the gospel message they have been studying, to rededicate themselves to be witnesses of the Resurrection of Jesus, and to go out, bearing the word of the gospel and with the light of Christ in their hands and their hearts. A suggested special Vigil Service marks the end of the course and the end of this book, and will hopefully provide an outline for such a celebration and vigil.

A companion book, published by Morehouse Publishing (USA), entitled *The Gospel Connection* and written by the same author, might helpfully be used as study material in conjunction with this book. Both books have been written as an offering to parish study groups who are seriously committed to preparing for the Decade of Evangelism.

Michael Marshall
St Louis, Mo. USA.

Evangelism and the Pentecost Event

EXPECTATION: EXPERIENCE: EXPLOSION: EXPLANATION: EXPANSION: EXPRESSION.

This Bible study can be used over any six-week period, but is ideally suited (because it was first specifically written) for the six weeks leading up to Pentecost. Its aim is quite clear: to be an aid in moving God's people from the celebration of Easter joy to a new commitment to Pentecost mission.

It is perhaps not an accident that although Lent, with the climax of Holy Week and Easter, is more extensively observed and celebrated by all the churches today; and although the winds of renewal are clearly blowing, bringing the joy of resurrection and the Easter experience to many parts of the body of Christ; there is still a sense of caution and restraint about the further and fuller claim of the gospel for Pentecost mission. The imperative for evangelism and mission has still to be fully owned by many Christians and many congregations today. So we will do well to give a new priority to Bible study during this period between Easter and Pentecost because we can do it in fellowship with Jesus and his disciples, who also appear to have given a special place to Bible study in those same weeks after the resurrection of Jesus (Luke 24:27, 32, 49). To that end — Pentecost — these Bible studies were written. They are intended for use either individually in personal, daily Bible study or by members of a Bible study group which meets each week.

The six themes which take us through our six weeks are as follows.

EXPECTATION: 'Stay in the city,' says Jesus, 'until you have been clothed with power from on high' (Luke 24:49); and again, also on the lips of Jesus — 'Do not leave Jerusalem, but wait for the gift my Father promised' (Acts 1:4). Our churches today need to recover a new sense of expectation and anticipation — not only for what God can do to empower those who wait upon him, but also to recover a new and greater expectation for growth and new members in our congregations.

EXPERIENCE: 'What does this mean?', they asked each other when they observed the apparently 'intoxicated' disciples emerging from that upper room on the day of Pentecost. Fear, with doors closed and firmly bolted (John 20:19), had now been overtaken by faith — a faith which had the power to open up all sorts of new possibilities. In that upper room, clearly, something had happened which brought about a change in the chemistry of life for those early disciples. Their experience could not easily be put into words, but that those disciples were moved (literally) was clearly apparent for all to see. Is the worship, preaching and teaching in our churches such that it moves people, enlightening their minds, warming their hearts and energizing their wills?

EXPLOSION: When men and women are baptised with Holy Spirit (like Jesus, at his baptism), 'immediately' the Spirit sends them 'out into the desert' — some god-forsaken place — to be the body of Christ and to confront Satan (as Jesus did) and to proclaim God's word (as Jesus did) and to witness to the true power of God in the face of principalities and powers — also as Jesus did.

The Holy Spirit drives the mission of the church, expelling us from the ghettos of fear and petty-mindedness into the larger world of God's kingdom to claim all nations as citizens of that kingdom.

EXPLANATION: Peter finds himself compelled to explain to a puzzled, amazed and surprised world the event of Pentecost. 'These men are not drunk, as you suppose. It's only nine in the morning.' For Christianity is an event, long before it is an idea. Something is happening in those early weeks of the life of the Christian church in Jerusalem. Good evangelistic witness seeks to answer the questions elicited by strange events — signs, wonders and apostolic acts

— manifested in the everyday life of the early, infant church. In our local church, is anything happening which demands explanation? Explosive events (apostolic acts) necessarily compel people to gossip and question in the market-place, speaking of the things we have seen and heard.

EXPANSION: 'And the Lord added to their number daily,' is a recurring chorus throughout Luke's record of the expansion of the early church. Clearly all of it was the Lord's work and the Lord's mission before it was the prime concern of the apostles. Here was no church growth for its own sake. Rather, the word was preached with power; ordinary folk told their stories of faith and gossiped the gospel. It was not long, therefore, before the Lord was touching the lives of hundreds of new Christians and adding these men and women to the local congregations — incorporating new disciples into the body of the apostolic church.

EXPRESSION: Those early Christians had no ecclesiastical self-consciousness. They did not set out with models and structures. The structures emerged out of the everyday life of men and women who 'devoted themselves to the apostles' teaching and to the fellowship, to the breaking of bread and to prayer'. Wherever there were cells expressing such patterns of everyday life, there was the church — the living body of Christ: Jesus in the skin of men and women — a living organism, before it was an organization. Furthermore, that church was not an end in itself. Rather, it was a means of bringing men and women into the true end and purpose of discipleship — into the fellowship of the citizens of the kingdom of God.

The record of apostolic acts or explosive events, as it moves from Easter joy to Pentecost mission, had all six of those signs — expectation, experience, explosion, explanation, expansion, expression. In heart, mind and spirit may those of us who run the course of this Bible study through Easter towards Pentecost move ever more closely and with ever deeper commitment into mission — and therefore necessarily into becoming evangelistic agents in and for God's world today.

St Luke, The Book of Acts and the Church Today

The book of the Acts of the Apostles is a special resource book within the New Testament for those who are seeking the renewal of God's church and the evangelization of the world. This is so for special reasons. It is the assumption of this slim volume that St Luke, the author of the gospel that bears his name and the author of the book of the Acts of the Apostles are, all three, one-and-the-same person. If that is so, then it means that the Acts of the Apostles is the one book in the New Testament which was written by a Gentile writer. Such an author necessarily brings — and possibly intentionally — a wider perspective on the missionary implications of the gospel, which was initially, at least, conceived in an exclusively Jewish context. As we watch that early, infant church breaking out of the mould of Jewish thinking and Jewish culture, we are observing the vital processes necessarily involved in the culturally-captive sect of Judaism becoming an open-ended, catholic church for all nations and all cultures.

The kingdom of God, which formed the core of the preaching and ministry of Jesus, was embodied in, and expressed itself initially through, the culture of Judaism. In order to do that, it had to both affirm, challenge and bend that culture, while at the same time expressing itself through the language and thought-forms of Judaism. It was never an easy process.

Then in the course of the mission of the early church there was further friction, as the teaching about the kingdom of God moved out of the mould of Judaism into the mould of the Greek-speaking world. Here again, like Cinderella's shoe, it did not fit all that well. If the gospel had been a scandal to Jews at the beginning, it was now certainly found to be foolishness to Greeks. The task of a missionary church, therefore, is two-fold. First, it needs to unscramble the mix and mould in which the teaching of the kingdom was first received: for the kingdom cannot be received naked without cultural clothing of some kind, but we need to know exactly what constitutes the Body and what is mere clothing. That is the first task.

The second is to know what can be embraced in the new culture which is being evangelized and what has to be challenged, converted and, if need be, radically re-ordered.

Luke has recorded this process and we have the privilege along with Theophilus, to whom Acts is dedicated, of watching the gospel of the kingdom as it first addresses the culture of Palestine in volume one (the gospel of Luke) and then of observing that same gospel of the kingdom addressing the culture of the Greek-speaking world of the Roman Empire.

In volume one the marriage is not easy and results in the death and victimization of the One Victim, once for all; while in volume two we see first Stephen, then James, Paul and the many others fall foul of a cultural resistance to the message of the kingdom.

In every age of missionary activity we see this process of cultural challenge taking place. Of course this is inevitable, because the priorities of the kingdom of this world and the priorities of the kingdom of God are radically different. It is true that they overlap at different points and in different places, but sooner or later, missionary movements go one of two ways. Either the church is captivated and falls captive to the secular culture of the world around it, slowly being domesticated and with its backbone slowly being filleted. In that case the challenge to the surrounding culture is minimized. Or it goes the other way. In the second case the culture is both challenged and changed to conform to the priorities of God's kingdom. As we observe this process we are compelled to 'judge for' ourselves, 'whether it is right in God's sight to' follow the prevailing winds of a passing culture or the eternal message of the kingdom of God (Acts 4:19).

The churches in the west today are necessarily moving from a position of maintenance to a policy of mission. In many ways the church forms the cultural skin of the kingdom of God. The profile, colouring and bearing of the church, while never totally conforming to the kingdom of God, nevertheless bear a remarkable and universal family likeness — such a church is the church 'at all times and in all places'. At the same time, however, the skin of the kingdom will be wonderfully diverse and locally distinctive. Language-forms and the forms of its worship will vary enormously, creating a rich universal orchestra of differing qualities of sound. So we are able in Luke's second volume to observe Paul's message of the kingdom, at first addressed to the Jews and in the synagogues and then to the Greeks, in Athens, Corinth and further afield.

In every situation, Paul's audience is asked to repent in words which call upon their hearers to change their outlook, to have second thoughts and to re-order their priorities. So at the Council of Jerusalem, the leaders of the early church had the difficult task of distinguishing between the gospel and the Jewish baggage in which they had first imported it before that same gospel could in its turn be exported to other cultures, in different packaging. For what we see is Paul, a Roman citizen, choosing nevertheless to live as a resident alien, whose true commonwealth was in heaven. In his turn therefore he calls upon his hearers to sit lightly to their rights as citizens of this world and to claim their baptismal rights by grace, together with a new identity — the identity of resident aliens, green cards and all. It would seem that Luke is anxious to show to Theophilus (whoever he may have been) that Paul and therefore the early Christians, while being necessarily resident aliens, could also be — and would firmly wish to be — responsible citizens of the Roman Empire. In many ways that is the ground-bass of the book of the Acts of the Apostles and it is a theme we do well to learn and study as the churches today, both in the north and west as well as in the developing countries, recover a new priority for mission and evangelism.

Hopefully we shall not make the same mistake as the reformers in the sixteenth century however — they got the argument the wrong way round. We shall not say that if something in church life is not to be found in the pages of scripture and its record of the early church, then it must be discarded. That is not the way to relate the life of the early church to missionary strategy today. However, hopefully we shall wish to observe that early church, exploding with evangelistic energy, and to see whether there are some essential ingredients in its life which are missing in our gospel life today. Where that is the case, we shall need to ask, 'Why are such ingredients absent in our local church?' and to recognize that in some cases there may well be a good reason for this. If no good reason can be found however, then we shall need the courage and the commitment to recover the characteristics of that first love — the infectious life of the early church. Decaffeinated Christianity is wonderful if you wish to sleep soundly! But today, God is calling his church afresh to wake up. He is stirring his people to new enterprises, to be workers together with him as he seeks to renew and refresh his church to be an effective witness to the kingdom of God — the whole gospel, for the whole church to the whole world.

We see something of that catholicity in Luke's book of Acts and we do well to read, mark, learn and inwardly digest it, for the renewal of the Lord's church today. For only a renewed church, truly ecumenical and genuinely international, can evangelize the whole world — 'all nations . . . to the ends of the earth'.

In fact, Luke's second volume was not called *the* book of *the* Acts of *the* Apostles. In the original title in Greek there are not all those definite articles: Acts of Apostles, or Apostolic Acts might be a more accurate translation therefore. This particular author's lust for alliteration tempts him to suggest a paraphrase for the title — what about 'Explosive Events'?

For the gospel, like new wine, refuses finally to be contained by any bottle — whether it be old or new, since it is not long before what is new becomes old. Language, thought-forms, vogues and attitudes form the old order which is passing away; and it is this world-view to which we are encouraged to sit lightly in the teaching of Jesus. There is something necessarily elusive then about the kingdom of God, because in the end it is too large to be contained by the limitations of this universe, however vast this universe may seem to be to our parochial vision. New wine demands renewed wine-skins if the kingdom of this world is eventually to become the kingdom of our Christ and of his God. And frankly Luke, and his hero Paul, would refuse to let us settle for anything less than that in the horizons of mission and evangelism.

Expectation   Week 1

The Christian should be schooled to expect the unexpected because, for those 'with eyes to see', the universe is littered with God's surprises. How else can it be for those who are committed to a faith which is built upon the premise of the resurrection? They went to the tomb on that first Easter morning, expecting to find death and yet they discovered life in the last place on earth you would ever expect to look for life — namely, the grave-yard. So the tomb was not after all the end, for them, but rather the womb of a new beginning. New life, in the place of the old, was the beginning of a new chapter of contradictions for those confused disciples. Jesus had spent three years trying to teach those disciples to expect the unexpected, to see the whole world from a new perspective — the perspective of the resurrection. Once they had witnessed for themselves the ultimate contradiction in the empty tomb, they then had to wait (with expectations) for the ultimate gift: the gift of God himself, giving himself in the person of his own Holy Spirit, to take over their lives with such power that in the future nothing would seem impossible. Nothing less than such an outlook on life would enable them to do the unexpected, to achieve the impossible and so to turn the world upside down and inside out with their teaching.

The trouble with our church today is that we no longer attempt the impossible — let alone expect the unexpected. We live by the cautious spirit of the age: market research, feasibility studies and working parties colour the life of the contemporary church. Unlike Abraham (the very opposite in fact), we never set out unless we know exactly where we are going, what it will look like when we get there and with sufficient supplies on board to make sure that we shall want for nothing on arrival. Even a weather forecast will tell us what we can reasonably expect to wear on arrival.

'Apart from me you can do nothing,' Jesus warns us. The trouble is that unless you undertake the impossible you will never prove the truth of that warning. We shall 'soldier on' in our own strength with our own programmes for maintenance, never disappointed too much because we had never hoped for too much.

Now read the record of the early, infant church, starting out with no resources (humanly speaking) to achieve the utterly impossible. Every day they proved for themselves the power of God in their weakness until they really began to live always expecting the unexpected. After all he who had died was raised from death — now *anything* after that (AD) was possible.

Before we can set out into a decade of evangelism, God's people need to raise their expectations to apostolic level. Imperceptibly, we fall back into the sort of life which is at best survival and maintenance and at worst a living death. Even the notice boards on our churches, the content of the parish bulletin, and the way we conduct worship on a Sunday, should tell us (if we could see it any longer) that we do not expect any new members in our churches — next Sunday. We do not expect our prayers to be answered and when they are, we attribute the answer to our prayers to economic, social or psychological factors. Do we expect new converts and what would we do with them if they turned up out of the blue? Rather we hoard, scratch and save our parish finances; we are pleased when we have put something away for a rainy day so that we shall not have to rely on anybody — not even God.

So great expectations must overtake our cautious calculations and teach us to live in the new way — God's way: dependence upon him upon whom all things depend. We must learn to live expecting to be surprised by God's generosity, grace and power at work in our everyday life — from the big things (like moving mountains) to small things (like the hairs on our head; or considering the lilies of the field) — *before* we consider our bank statements and *always* with the empty tomb as that which is determinative of the shape of things to come. For in the end, 'all things', indeed, 'work together for good for those who love God'.

Questions for reflection during the week and for discussion in the group

1.   How much of our faith is fear masquerading as faith?
     How much of our life is built on superstition rather than a personal, daily dependence upon the sufficiency of God's grace?
2.   Do we read 'our stars'? If so, can we tease out our motives for astrology, hand-reading and superstition?
3.   In what way should expecting the unexpected colour our morning prayers?
4.   Is our church programme, in every detail, primarily for new-comers?

Great Expectations

On one occasion, while [Jesus] was eating with [the apostles], he gave them this command: 'Do not leave Jerusalem, but wait for the gift my Father promised, which you have heard me speak about. For John baptised with water, but in a few days you will be baptised with the Holy Spirit.'

So when they met together, they asked him, 'Lord, are you at this time going to restore the kingdom to Israel?'

He said to them: 'It is not for you to know the times or dates the Father has set by his own authority. But you will receive power when the Holy Spirit comes on you; and you will be my witnesses in Jerusalem, and in all Judea and Samaria, and to the ends of the earth.'

Acts 1:4—8

Luke tells us that Jesus, during those 'forty days', schooled his apostles in three main areas: the scriptures, the Holy Spirit and the kingdom. We know from the last chapter of Luke's gospel, that Jesus spent time both 'opening' the scriptures to them, and 'opening their minds' to the scriptures (Luke 24:32, 45). He taught them about the gift of the Holy Spirit (Acts 1:4–5) and the empowerment for ministry and witness which would come from that gift. And above all he taught them about the kingdom. (v. 3b).

But notice that the apostles clearly misunderstood most of what Jesus told them — certainly about the kingdom of God and the Holy Spirit. They lacked perception and perspective when they asked, 'Are you at this time going to restore the kingdom to Israel?' It was John Calvin who commented on this verse that 'there are as many errors in this question as words' (*Institutes* I). The use of the word 'restore' would indicate that the apostles were still thinking in terms of a territorial kingdom of the old Israel, liberated through the 'power' of politics and force from Roman occupation. Furthermore, that kingdom was limited in their vision to Israel in the nationalistic sense. Finally the phrase 'at this time' shows that the apostles could see no further than the end of their lifespan. In spite of all that Jesus had taught them and showed them, their minds were closed, their vision was parochial and their God was too small by half. Yet Jesus, the patient teacher, is true to his word: 'I have much more to say to you, more than you can now bear. But when he, the Spirit of truth, comes, he will guide you into all truth' (John 16:12f).

The kingdom of God is not territorial: you will never find it on any map, except the map of the human heart. Like those two disciples on the road to Emmaus, the apostles could only see redemption and salvation in terms of the political kingdom of Israel. Luke, as a writer and traveller, had grasped the catholic and universal nature of the kingdom. It is interesting that he is the only New Testament writer who insists upon calling the Sea of Galilee 'a lake'. For him, a sea meant at least something of the proportions of the Mediterranean — nothing less!

For the kingdom of God knows no national boundaries. So the words of Jesus in reply to the disciples' question are deliberately pointed. The apostles were to include rather than to exclude the land of the despised Samaritans on their pilgrimage of witness from Jerusalem to the 'ends of the earth'. The kingdom of God, like new wine, cannot be contained in the old way of seeing things and it is essentially a long-term investment. It is always 'urgent' which is not the same thing as 'immediate'. Nearly all the parables of the kingdom on the lips of Jesus speak of steady growth and long-term harvest.

However, Jesus has complete trust in the power of the Holy Spirit to lead expectant disciples into the fullness of truth and furthermore to empower them to witness to that truth — he has great expectations! He does not need to hammer home the full implications of the geography of catholic mission. Rather he leaves that to the working of the Holy Spirit later — through the dream of Peter at Joppa and the deliberations of the apostles at Jerusalem . . . They could not have 'borne it' at that stage.

EXPERIENCE

A church which is preparing for a new chapter of evangelistic mission will do well to place Bible study and teaching about the Holy Spirit and the kingdom of God at the top of its agenda.

The apostolic church 'waited', we are told, upon the Lord. It may be necessary for us to retreat before we can advance. An annual parish retreat to wait upon the Lord and to seek that further empowerment of the Holy Spirit is strategic in all plans for evangelism.

Jesus had spelt out the universality of the kingdom at the very outset in his mandate for mission — Jerusalem, Judea and Samaria and to the ends of the earth. Yet, they were too deaf to hear it and too blind to see it. The church today needs to increase 'daily in the Holy Spirit more and more', which means, in practical terms, a constant commitment to prayer and Bible study. Otherwise our vision will be cramped, our commitment conditional and our God will be too small.

For there are no 'no-go' areas for mission and evangelism. 'Samaria' is always included. Often it is right on our doorstep and the most difficult to see as a field ready for harvest. Who or what is our 'Samaria'? For it is at just that point that we most need the empowerment of the Holy Spirit and the larger perspective of the kingdom of God.

The Right Expectations?

MONDAY   **WEEK 1**

Now a man crippled from birth was being carried to the temple gate called Beautiful, where he was put every day to beg from those going into the temple courts. When he saw Peter and John about to enter, he asked them for money. Peter looked straight at him, as did John. Then Peter said, 'Look at us!' So the man gave them his attention, expecting to get something from them.

Then Peter said, 'Silver or gold I do not have, but what I have I give you. In the name of Jesus Christ of Nazareth, walk.' Taking him by the right hand, he helped him up, and instantly the man's feet and ankles became strong. He jumped to his feet and began to walk. Then he went with them into the temple courts, walking and jumping, and praising God.

Acts 3:2—8

The scene is set at the main, eastern entrance to the great temple of Herod in Jerusalem. You enter the temple precincts from the court of the Gentiles, via the Nicanor Gate, which most commentators agree is the gate to which Luke is referring to as 'the Beautiful Gate'. If this were that gate, then indeed it was a splendid and beautiful entrance to the temple. Josephus the Jewish historian tells us that this gate 'greatly excelled those that were only covered over with silver and gold' (*The Jewish Wars* V.53). It was huge and impressive in proportions, with massive double doors. By contrast with this splendour, magnificence and opulence, the crippled beggar sits begging.

Luke is anxious to tell us that this man was chronically paralysed and had to be carried, and furthermore that his was a congenital case. Forty years old, he had been crippled from birth: a particularly hopeless case.

He asks Peter and John for money, probably never even looking at them. He was only interested in the gift and not the givers. Peter insists however that the man looks straight at them and at once the drama moves from the impersonal to the personal. 'I do not have *anything* to give you', says Peter. 'I only have some *body* to give — Jesus of Nazareth. In his name, I command you to stand up and walk.'

Then Peter took him by the hand, as he had seen Jesus do in the story of Jairus' daughter, also recorded by Luke (Luke 8:54) and helped the man to his feet. In fulfilment of the prophecy of Isaiah, the man not only walks, but leaps and jumps for joy: 'Then will the lame leap like a deer' (Isaiah 35:6).

EXPLANATION

Thomas Walker says of this passage: 'The power was Christ's but the hand was Peter's.' The first volume is about the ministry of Jesus of Nazareth, doing the will of his Father through his earthly incarnate body in Palestine by the power of the Holy Spirit. The second volume of Luke (Acts) is also about the ministry of the same Jesus of Nazareth, who also by the power of the Holy Spirit is working through his earthly sacramental body which is also here to do the will of the Father not only in Palestine but to the ends of the earth, as it is already being done perfectly in heaven.

So in the name (and therefore, in Jewish thought, in the power) of Jesus Christ of Nazareth, the apostles are confident that they can continue to do the work that they saw Jesus do during his earthly ministry — and 'even greater things than these', because he has gone 'to the Father' and the Holy Spirit has been given to them (John 14:12 and 7:39). So why is this so surprising (Acts 3:12)? The power that is at work here is not the personal property of Peter or John but rather the same power that had been at work in their midst at the hands of Jesus, whose name and memory were still very much present in Jerusalem.

EXPERIENCE

This same power for salvation and healing is given to the apostolic church in every generation. For the human problem is indeed congenital — original sin is a radical disease. The solution must be equally radical. It stems not from talents and skills inherited in our genes but from the gift of the Holy Spirit when we are 'born again' in our baptism. Firstly we must be convinced afresh that what people need and what they are crying out for is not the same as what they say they want. The man *wanted* money; he *needed* salvation. The tragedy of mankind is that we have mistaken the creation for the creator. But the church has fallen into the same trap and so often gives people stones when they need bread — the bread of life. All dependencies are a craving for God in disguise. The church needs to focus that dependency upon the *One* upon whom all things depend.

Secondly we need to remember as a church today that the power to do the works of Christ is a gift — of the Holy Spirit. We receive that gift when we become a people of the first beatitude: 'Blessed are those who know their need of God' (NEB Matthew 5:3). We need to come empty handed to a generous and loving Father who knows our needs before we ask, for he is the giver of all good gifts. Only so shall we discover the power of the gospel, that having nothing we can possess all things.

Fasting, poverty of spirit and emptiness of self-sufficiency all constitute the necessary prologues to all apostolic acts of power and are a necessary preparation for evangelism and mission. For the human problem is not a financial one — silver and gold — but one of faith; and the solution is to be found not in any power we acquire but rather in the power of the Spirit which can only be given.

The Same Expectations As Before

TUESDAY   **WEEK 1**

In Joppa there was a disciple named Tabitha (which, when translated, is Dorcas), who was always doing good and helping the poor. About that time she became sick and died, and her body was washed and placed in an upstairs room. Lydda was near Joppa; so when the disciples heard that Peter was in Lydda, they sent two men to him, 'Please come at once!'

Peter went with them, and when he arrived he was taken upstairs to the room. All the widows stood around him, crying and showing him the robes and other clothing that Dorcas had made while she was still with them.

Peter sent them all out of the room; then he got down on his knees and prayed. Turning towards the dead woman, he said, 'Tabitha, get up.' She opened her eyes, and seeing Peter she sat up. He took her by the hand and helped her to her feet. Then he called the believers and the widows and presented her to them alive. This became known all over Joppa, and many people believed in the Lord.

Acts 9:36—42

In chapter nine, Luke recalls a pair of miracles worked through the apostle Peter. They are presented in an almost exemplary way as if to show that Peter was truly an apostle and therefore, in the words of Paul, did 'the things that mark an apostle — signs, wonders and miracles' (2 Corinthians 12:12).

First Peter healed Aeneas, a paralytic who had been bedridden for eight years (Acts 9:32—34). Then he raised from the dead Tabitha (in the Greek 'Dorcas', which means 'gazelle').

We need to notice that in both cases Peter deliberately imitates the deeds and even the very words of Jesus, which he had heard and seen during the days of Christ's earthly ministry in Palestine. In the case of Aeneas, the words used by Peter are deliberately reminiscent of the words used by Jesus, when he healed the paralytic in Capernaum (Mark 2:1ff and Luke 5:17ff) — 'Get up and take up your mat'. Furthermore in both cases the word for healing used both by Peter and by Jesus is the word *anastēthi* — the word used for resurrection. God raised up Jesus from the dead. He still raises up all who are in Christ.

But the parallels are even yet more striking. Read again the story of the raising of Jairus' daughter (Mark 5:35—43). Men come to Jesus to tell him of the death of the young girl: men are sent to Peter to ask him to come to Joppa. On arrival at the house of Jairus, 'Jesus saw a commotion, with people crying and wailing loudly', and he 'put them all out'. When Peter arrived at the house of Tabitha, 'all the widows stood around him, crying' and Peter also 'sent them all out of the room'. Then, Jesus 'took her by the hand', and Peter also 'took her by the hand'. Jesus said '*Talitha koum*' in the Aramaic; Peter said '*Tabitha koum*', if he also, as he probably did, spoke in

Aramaic. There is only a difference of one letter between the two words of salvation, healing and resurrection on the lips of Peter and Jesus.

EXPLANATION

Of course Peter, along with James and John, had been party to the most remarkable healing miracles of Jesus: they had seen the ministry of Jesus Christ at first hand. It is hardly surprising that Peter would 'catch' words, phrases and actions from the master. We need, however, to notice one vital difference between the two miracles. Luke deliberately records that before addressing the dead Tabitha, Peter 'got on his knees and prayed'. Jesus does not in the story of the raising of Jairus' daughter. Furthermore, Peter is quite explicit when he heals Aeneas: 'Jesus Christ heals you' he says, not Peter.

Both miracles are performed by Jesus Christ. Peter is the apostolic instrument in the hands of the heavenly Christ who is still interceding for us and ministering to us through his sacramental body, the church.

EXPERIENCE

'We think too much of what we can do,' says William Barclay, 'and too little of what Christ can do through us.' Does our church rely solely upon the power of God, to anoint a word of power which in turn will accomplish what God is seeking to do in and for the world, through his apostolic church? Notice the place of the men who go to plead the case of the needy both before Jesus and before Peter. We need today a powerful army of intercessors (often the widows and old women of the church). We need a new obedience to his word and a new love of the words of Jesus. We need a new experience of the power of the anointed word in preaching and in ministry. We need above all a new expectation concerning the power in the very name of Jesus.

'With God all things are possible,' says the angel to the expectant Mary. That must be the source and root of all our confidence in accomplishing the mighty works that God gives to his people in every age. And what are these works? Essentially they are the works of salvation: to raise up the downcast, the sinner, the diseased, and to know with all our hearts that there is no other name given under heaven whereby we may be healed, than the precious and powerful name of Jesus. We shall only preach an effective word of power or minister with power (even over death) if we, like Peter, are first brought to our knees. 'Without him we cannot: without us he will not' (Augustine).

Expecting the Unexpected

Then Peter came to himself and said, 'Now I know without a doubt that the Lord sent his angel and rescued me from Herod's clutches and from everything the Jewish people were anticipating.'

When this had dawned on him, we went to the house of Mary the mother of John, also called Mark, where many people had gathered and were praying. Peter knocked at the outer entrance, and a servant girl named Rhoda came to answer the door. When she recognised Peter's voice, she was so overjoyed she ran back without opening it and exclaimed, 'Peter is at the door!'

'You're out of your mind,' they told her. When she kept insisting that it was so, they said, 'It must be his angel.'

But Peter kept on knocking, and when they opened the door and saw him, they were astonished. Peter motioned with his hand for them to be quiet and described how the Lord had brought him out of prison. 'Tell James and the brothers about this,' he said, and then he left for another place.

Acts 12:11—17

The prelude to this apostolic event, is the earnest prayer of the church (verse 5). Luke uses the same word for earnest, unremitting or fervent, as he used to describe the passionate prayer of Jesus in the Garden of Gethsemane (Luke 22:44). When Jesus was praying on that Thursday evening before his crucifixion, he was entering into the battle for the world, and therefore into battle with evil, not merely flesh and blood, but rather principalities and powers and the rulers of darkness.

So it is in this account. John Stott writes: 'Here then were the two great communities, the world and the church, arrayed against one another, each wielding an appropriate weapon. On the one side was the authority of Herod, the power of the sword and the security of the prison. On the other side, the church turned to prayer, which is the only power which the powerless possess.'

Notice also that Peter is asleep. James had already been beheaded and Jesus had prophesied to Peter that he would die a martyr's death (John 21:18). Yet Peter has sufficient trust to be sound asleep. God can often do more for us when we are asleep — because we do not get in the way so much!

Then when the prayers of the church are answered, the irony is that they do not believe that Peter is knocking at the door. Rather, they prefer any other explanation for this unexpected turn-around of events.

The prayers of the faithful win the day! 'The prayer of a righteous man avails much,' James tells us in his epistle. The weapons of this world (even an extra-careful prison procedure — verse six) proved to be powerless against the powerful prayers of faith. Herod's plans are defeated and as though to hammer this point home, Luke concludes this whole section with the story of an untimely and ugly death for Herod (verses 21ff).

'Now war arose in heaven' (Revelation 12:7). We sometimes forget that we are not simply engaged in a discussion group, or a conference, but rather in a full-scale cosmic war and that when we seek to evangelize or to speak the truth, the Evil One is at work still (in spite of the victory of Calvary) to overturn the church and to silence the gospel. Our battle is not simply against flesh and blood — and therefore the image of the church as an army is more appropriate than the image of a discussion group. The weapons we wield, however, are not the same as those of the world. We need to put on the whole armour of God as it is listed in the epistle to the Ephesians (6:11ff). The weapons the world uses to spread its perverted gospel are formidable indeed: powerful advertising, subliminal suggestion, big money, the technology of communication. It is not inappropriate to speak of the world's evangelistic crusade but we must realize also that we are in similar ways involved in a crusade and we need to prepare for it with fervent, continuous and expectant prayer. For this sort does not come out except by prayer and fasting (Mark 9:29).

EXPERIENCE

As in the Old Testament story of David and Goliath, it is David who appears as powerless while Goliath seems to have all the weapons and experience of power on his side. The reverse of course is true. It is to the powerless that God gives his power. All prayer is a gift of God, for we do not even know how to pray let alone to pray effectively.

But do we make the connections between prayer fervently offered and God's deliverance? Do we see the church in the Soviet Union today as delivered from imprisonment and oppression in answer to the prayers of the faithful? Do we see it as a miracle of God in our time? Doors *have* opened, seemingly of their own accord. Someone may list all the other human and economic factors, but Christ's people who have prayed for so long should be ready to give God the glory, to give thanks and to recall another mighty act of God in the deliverance of his people through the power of earnest prayer. We should not enter into the battle for the soul, which we call evangelism, either without the power of earnest and fervent prayer and fasting nor without a renewed faith in the Lord of history. Only so can we begin to expect the unexpected at the hand of God in our day.

Expectant Prayer

THURSDAY   **WEEK 1**

In the church at Antioch there were prophets and teachers: Barnabas, Simeon called Niger, Lucius of Cyrene, Manaen (who had been brought up with Herod the tetrarch) and Saul. While they were worshipping the Lord and fasting, the Holy Spirit said, 'Set apart for me Barnabas and Saul for the work to which I have called them.' So after they had fasted and prayed, they placed their hands on them and sent them off.

The two of them, sent on their way by the Holy Spirit, went down to Seleucia and sailed from there to Cyprus. When they arrived at Salamis, they proclaimed the word of God in the Jewish synagogues.

Acts 13:1—5a

EVENT

Now we come to the great turning point in the book of Acts. In the first twelve chapters Luke has recorded the witness of the early church 'in Jerusalem' and 'in all Judea' and in the no-go area of Samaria. Now, in obedience to the missionary mandate given by

Jesus to his apostles in the opening chapter, the fragile church must expand its evangelistic expectations, because the church that lives to itself dies by itself.

What better place for the church to capture something of that catholic, world-wide vision than at Antioch? Just look at the variety and catholicity of that cell of the church in Antioch. Barnabas was a Jew from Cyprus — 'a Levite' according to Luke's earlier, exact description (4:36). Then there was Simeon (clearly a Hebrew name) who was black — probably a black African, and almost certainly St Simeon of Cyrene, the black African who carried the cross of Jesus: the father of Alexander and Rufus, also well-known in the early church and in Pauline circles (Mark 15:21 and Romans 16:13). (How could anyone who had carried the cross of Jesus not end up becoming a Christian, whether they carried voluntarily or had no choice?) Lucius certainly came from North Africa, while Manaen had aristocratic connections in Herod's court. Saul, the fifth-named church leader at Antioch, was from the most prestigious university city of Tarsus, an orthodox and trained rabbi by background. What a collection! 'Men from many lands and many backgrounds had discovered the secret of "togetherness"', says Barclay, 'because they had discovered the secret of Christ.'

Yet it has to be said that they had discovered the right kind of 'togetherness'. The catholic church ought to be a group of people who, as far as you can see, have nothing whatever in common, except the One through whom they hold all things in common — even the catholic Christ, the Man for others.

The Lord had blessed that warm group of church leaders at Antioch with a rich fellowship. Yet according to Luke (verse 3), it was this very warm and closely knit fellowship, which after laying hands on Paul and Barnabas, 'sent them off'. As a matter of fact, possibly a better translation (as in the New English Bible) for the verb *apoluō* would be the phrase 'let them go'!

It was Archbishop William Temple who used to say that the church was the only society which existed for the sake of those who were not members of it. Real love does not seek the cosy comfort of the club and clique mentality. Love goes out of its way. So since the time of Abraham, God has been sending carefully chosen people, empowered with ample resources of grace, on the most impossible errands to the most unlikely places and to the most unpromising people. We call it mission. It originates in the heart of the communion and fellowship of the Blessed Trinity. In these last days, God has so loved that he has put himself out and 'sent his Son'. And all this is the work of Love — the Holy Spirit of God. So at the baptism of Jesus, the moment of anointing by the Holy Spirit is the same moment as the expulsion of Jesus, driven by love and for love, into the desert for confrontation with evil, for ministry and mission.

EXPERIENCE

I suppose we would regard that little church at Antioch as being very renewed! Certainly it was richly graced with the gifts of ministry among its leadership. Yet notice what renewal and the gifts of the Holy Spirit are intended to lead us to. The Holy Spirit is given to his church to renew and refresh it, but then to break it open. All gifts are given to be given away: not closeted and hoarded.

The renewed church today has lost its way. 'The church that prays together, stays together'. Yes, but it must not stop there! 'The church that stays together, decays together.' We must know how to move from the joy of Easter resurrection and renewal to the mission of Pentecost. 'As the Father has sent me, I am sending you' (John 20:21). The gifts of the Holy Spirit are always given for mission. We must always let go of what we have been given if we wish to keep it for ever. Only so will the mandate for mission 'to the ends of the earth' be realized. There will come a moment in the life of every growing congregation when we must divide the congregation and let some of them go to start another mission.

Changing Our Expectations

From Troas we put out to sea and sailed straight for Samothrace, and the next day on to Neapolis. From there we travelled to Philippi, a Roman colony and the leading city of that district of Macedonia. And we stayed there several days.

On the Sabbath we went outside the city gate to the river, where we expected to find a place of prayer. We sat down and began to speak to the women who had gathered there. One of those listening was a woman named Lydia, a dealer in purple cloth from the city of Thyatira, who was a worshipper of God. The Lord opened her heart to respond to Paul's message. When she and the members of her household were baptised, she invited us to her home. 'If you consider me a believer in the Lord,' she said, 'come and stay at my house.' And she persuaded us.

Acts 16:11—15

EVENT

It would seem that in Philippi there was no synagogue. In order to have a synagogue in Judaism there had to be a minimum of ten male members. Luke records that there were only women present at the place of prayer, situated outside the city gates. Wherever Jews were unable to have a synagogue they would generally designate 'places of prayer'. Usually these were located close to a river, which would be at hand for the various ceremonial washings so important in all eastern religions. The small river Gangites flowed near to this place of prayer just outside the large garrison city of Philippi.

Among the women sitting there, was Lydia, 'a dealer in purple cloth from the city of Thyatira'. Thyatira was the city famed for centuries for its purple dye. The purple dye — an extremely expensive product — would be gathered drop by drop from a particular shellfish. Lydia was clearly a wealthy woman and a merchant of some standing.

The Lord chose to open her heart to the message that Paul was preaching. All anointed preaching is the work of the Lord and has the capacity to open what Augustine calls the 'ears of the heart'.

So she and 'all her household', Luke tells us (as he does on three other occasions, 10:24; 16:33; 18:8) are all baptised. That would include not only slaves, but also possibly children, young people of all ages. It would include all those for whom she was responsible.

EXPLANATION

Luke purposely records that Paul and his companions (including Luke himself) set out expecting to find a place of prayer. They usually found the nearest synagogue in any city they visited. They might have said to each other: 'What a pity, there is no synagogue in Philippi! Where on earth can we start?'

They expected to find only a place of prayer. Instead they ended up finding and founding a house-church. 'Where two or three are gathered in my name,' Jesus says deliberately, 'there am I in the midst.' Jesus exploded the Old Testament view of what constituted a church or synagogue. Matthew 18:20 has the verb behind the word 'synagogue' and is saying in effect: 'In order to have a church you do not need ten men: just two or three gathered ('synagogued') in my name and there am I in all the fullness of the gospel.' That is the church.

So Paul and his band were surprised by joy. They had not expected to found a house-church on that day. However Lydia, like the good man of the house in the gospel accounts, offers to Paul as he did to Jesus, her home. A Christian is always given, as Paul reminds us, to hospitality. That is a ministry in itself. So, just like the jailer in Acts 16, baptism for Lydia also led straight into ministry and care for others (Acts 16:33—34).

Sometimes we are blinded by the negative. We must learn not to say that we have not got to hand this or that — a synagogue. Rather, we must have eyes to see what we have been given and then to use it. Those water pots, standing empty at the wedding feast of Cana at Galilee are worthy of our attention. The hosts did *not* have any wine, but they *did* have large, empty water pots. What more do you need?

We need to look in our parishes at all the gifts, people and resources that God has given to us and to take stock first, before ever we begin our evangelism. God will choose to work through what we have in place already and then he can lead us to the other place of his purposes — outside the gate of the city.

We must learn the confidence to preach and teach *outside* the church building. We must be ready to meet people where they are (like Lydia), in order to bring them where the Lord would have them be. The house-church is the place and environment where the Lord's word is being gladly heard today, and where renewal and refreshment are most effective — as in earlier times of Christian history. Are we ready to go outside the West door and the gates of our churches to where two or three are gathered? It is there that we so often find the waters of new life.

Beyond All Expectations

Just before dawn Paul urged them all to eat. 'For the last fourteen days,' he said, 'you have been in constant suspense and have gone without food — you haven't eaten anything. Now I urge you to take some food. You need it to survive. Not one of you will lose a single hair from his head.' After he said this, he took some bread and gave thanks to God in front of them all. Then he broke it and began to eat. They were all encouraged and ate some food themselves. Altogether there were 276 of us on board. When they had eaten as much as they wanted, they lightened the ship by throwing the grain into the sea.

When daylight came, they did not recognise the land, but they saw a bay with a sandy beach, where they decided to run the ship aground if they could.

Acts 27:33—39

EVENT

Paul takes charge. Throughout the drama of the shipwreck story as recorded in Acts, it is Paul who seems to be in charge rather than the sailors, the centurion or the prisoners. And because Paul is in charge, God is really in charge. 'All things are yours . . . and you are Christ's and Christ is God's' (1 Corinthians 3:21, 23). If Jesus is not Lord of all, he is not really Lord at all. Jesus is not only Lord of the church, he is Lord of history. So, reminiscent of our Lord's teaching about a God who is a Father with the whole world in his hands, Paul repeats to the whole 276-strong company on board words of assurance which again recall words of Jesus — 'Not one of you will lose a single hair from his head' (compare Matthew 10:30 — 'even the very hairs of your head are all numbered').

So Paul calms their fears; he demands that they all stay together and see it through together; and he encourages them to build up their strength by urging everyone to take some food.

Yet at the same time, he witnesses to his faith in Christ by publicly giving thanks to God and blessing the food. This passage may or may not indicate that he actually celebrated the Eucharist. However that may be, it does assert that Paul gave thanks to God publicly on the ship when the storm was blowing. He gave thanks — 'at all times and in all places'. He asserts the good news in the very midst of the bad news. He affirms confidence in God in the midst of fear. Against all odds, Paul is confident that 'all things work together for good to those who love God' (Romans 8:28).

EXPLANATION

Here is a picture of Paul the evangelist and missionary who is nonetheless concerned for the whole man. He ministers to the whole person — not just to the spiritual side of our needs. He is as concerned that sailors and prisoners should not be allowed to escape as he is that they should eat and build up their natural strength for the climax of the crisis when the ship will run aground and break up. Later he takes the initiative in gathering wood to keep the fire burning on the beach: a light and fire in the darkness and cold of the night.

For St Paul there were not two gospels: the gospel of salvation and the social gospel. Both were aspects of the same love of God for all mankind, made known to us in the person, message and ministry of Jesus. It is not a question for Paul of either/or: either we feed the hungry with food or we give them the Eucharist and the food of the Bread of Life. No, it is both/and.

EXPERIENCE

So we must not draw a line between mission and evangelism or between the social gospel and the gospel. The connection between the two is the same Jesus who is both fully human and fully divine. The same Jesus we worship in the consecrated bread in the sanctuary is the same Jesus we worship *in* the poor, *in* the homeless and *in* the hungry.

A Jesuit priest tells the story of his visit to the hospice of Mother Teresa in Calcutta. On Sunday morning, when giving the host of the eucharist to Mother Teresa, he was struck by the look of total love and adoration that swept across her face as she received the Body of Christ at the early morning Mass.

Later the same day, she showed him round the hospice. Standing in her little ward, she explained that this area was reserved for those closest to death and the most sick among the patients. Suddenly one man groaned in extreme pain. Mother Teresa left the priest for a moment, put her arm around the dying man and suddenly — there again, was that same look and expression of adoration and love as he had seen so distinctively on her face that morning at Mass.

Mother Teresa had made the connection between the Body of Christ on the altar and the body of Christ — the indwelling of Jesus in the poor, the needy and the people of the first beatitude. 'Whatever you did for one of the least of these brothers of mine, you did for me' (Matthew 25:40). St Paul made the connection, at all times and in all places — and in the last place on earth you would ever expect him to do so. Mother Teresa had made the connection — 'Christ in you, the hope of glory' (Colossians 1:27) — even where things seemed most hopeless. Countless Christians over the ages have made that connection. Have we?

If it's alive: it moves! A living church will be moved by preachers, prayer and above all by worship. And not only emotionally, but in every way. Only when you move (or are moved) do you begin to see different things differently and from a new point of view. Seeing things from a new point of view is exactly the translation of 'repentance' — or *metanoia* in Greek — so we can conclude: only a church which is moved by the word, by its worship and its witness will be a church which can repent and therefore have the capacity to change.

Yet Anglican Christians, especially, are afraid of what we call religious experience. They distrust it, feeling more secure if they can receive and retain their religion purely on the brain. Then of course they are not so likely to be out of control. Since the age of rationalism (since the eighteenth century) in the West, we have focussed all our experiences which we trust in the two inches or so above the eyes: all our investment is literally in our brains. Earlier generations have located the centre of our personality in our hearts, our chests and — especially the Jews — in our bowels and our guts. Furthermore they have not been afraid of deep experiences when they have expressed themselves in a psychosomatic way — tears, laughter, dancing, singing.

All deep experiences — not least religious experiences — express themselves through the body — any good doctor will tell you that. We cannot cope with purely spiritual experiences — but then we are not purely spiritual: we are not angels, and we never will be. When men and women experience God and the Holy Spirit through worship, prayer or preaching we are moved and that experience has to find physical and bodily expression. God cannot break through into our lives unless he first breaks down the barriers of resistance — not least the barriers of reason, so called common sense and proper conduct. Furthermore, we cannot surrender our lives while we are still in control, something has to give. <u>So when those first apostles were invaded by the Holy Spirit at Pentecost, they experienced a new reality in their lives taking control of them</u> — filling them with the life of God himself. That religious experience manifested itself in a bodily way — <u>so that sensible passers-by on that morning at nine o'clock thought they were drunk.</u> They spoke in tongues because they were filled with unspeakable joy: experience had overtaken eloquence.

All the saints in history tells us of their strange, and unnerving, experiences of God. They also teach us not to put too much store by them, because this experience business works two ways: religious experience expresses itself through the chemistry of the body; but, as we know, changes in body chemistry can also bring about disturbing and ecstatic experiences. We do not measure therefore holiness of life by any of these experiences but rather the repentance that such experiences enable and the change of heart and will which should follow upon any deep and authentic experience of God the Holy Spirit at work in our lives. <u>If we are really moved on Sunday morning it will show itself even on Monday morning.</u>

So our preaching, our prayers and our worship should indeed move people — move them to a change of heart and discretion; to repentance and to a new way of living. Is our worship such that it moves us into the kingdom each week as the priest invites us to be moved by the lifting up of our hearts to God in praise and prayer? Or do our minds immediately sit on that experience and keep it earthbound? True worship should invade all our senses. Music has a special part to play in this — but so do many other things in worship, for true worship must speak to all the senses.

Watch a child playing on the carpet, touching, smelling, tasting (literally) everything. We start life as natural 'catholics'; but slowly we are conditioned to become nice, disinfected, cerebral protestants ('Stop putting it in your mouth, darling'). Yet, 'taste and see how good the Lord is', say the psalmists, and they should know about religious experience all right!

And so with our preaching. It will just go in one ear and out of the other if it is nothing more than a religious lecture. And so also with our prayers. Unless we are willing to use our bodies in prayer and worship, standing, sitting, walking, prostrating, kneeling, crossing ourselves or with hands extended or praising and praying with hands in the air — always empty yet waiting to be filled in every way (hence fasting) by a generous and gracious God — unless this is so, then of course our minds will wander! So in the book of Acts, they did not only believe in God: rather he was their deepest experience. They experienced him in confusing and embarrassing ways, always in ways which showed them, in no uncertain way, who was really in control. The principal person in the book of Acts is not Peter, James or Paul — but Jesus. It is his church, his Spirit is in control and it is he who gives to men and women a new compulsion for mission and a new motivation to do the will of the Father on earth as it is perfectly being done in heaven.

Questions for reflection during the week and for discussion in the group

1.　Where, when and how have I experienced God in my life?
　　Did it make any difference?
　　Do I keep a spiritual journal?
2.　Is our Sunday worship such that it 'speaks' to all kinds of people — the blind, the deaf and those with or without university degrees?
3.　What about the preaching?
　　Is it an essay or an event?
　　Is it only information or does it move us with aspiration?
4.　Where, when and how do I spend my time for personal prayer each day? What can we do about 'wandering thoughts'?

An Amazing and Perplexing Experience

Now there were staying in Jerusalem God-fearing Jews from every nation under heaven. When they heard this sound, a crowd came together in bewilderment, because each one heard them speaking in his own language. Utterly amazed, they asked: 'Are not all these men who are speaking Galileans? Then how is it that each one of us hears them in his own native language? Parthians, Medes and Elamites; residents of Mesopotamia, Judea and Cappadocia, Pontus and Asia, Phrygia and Pamphylia, Egypt and the parts of Libya near Cyrene; visitors from Rome (both Jews and converts to Judaism); Cretans and Arabs — we hear them declaring the wonders of God in our own tongues!' Amazed and perplexed, they asked one another, 'What does this mean?'

Acts 2:5—12

EVENT

There were three great festivals in the Jewish calendar: the Passover, Pentecost and the Feast of Tabernacles. All male Jews living within twenty miles of Jerusalem were required to come to Jerusalem and to the temple for these three festivals. Pentecost was celebrated just fifty days after the Passover and therefore most years it occurred at the beginning of June. Travelling conditions at that time of the year were at their best and therefore there would never be a day in the year when there would be a larger or more international crowd gathered in Jerusalem than on the feast of Pentecost.

This feast had two main emphases. It celebrated the giving of the law of Moses on Mount Sinai, reckoned in Jewish tradition to have occurred just fifty days after the Exodus. Pentecost also celebrated harvest thanksgiving, the ingathering of the crops and first fruits which were offered to God: the first omer of barley and two loaves. As such it was a public holiday and the streets of Jerusalem would be filled to capacity with crowds of Jews who had come from all over the known world around the Mediterranean basin.

What a day then for the birthday of the Christian church! On that day we read (Acts 2:41) that three thousand souls were added to the small band of Christians — the harvesting of the first fruits had begun. 'The time was come to put in the sickle of the word,' wrote John Chrysostom, 'for here, as the sickle, keen-edged, came the Spirit down' (*Homily* IV).

Furthermore, the new law, the *novum mandatum*, was to be written not in stone, but rather in fulfilment of the ancient prophecy, 'I will write my law in their inward hearts': they experienced the love of God shed abroad in their hearts.

EXPLANATION

Yet together with that multiracial crowd, we also need to ask, 'What does this mean?' Theologically, it is fairly clear what it means: 'A deliberate and dramatic reversal of the curse of Babel,' writes John Stott. 'At Babel human languages were confused and the nations were scattered; in Jerusalem the language barrier was supernaturally overcome as a sign that the nations would now be gathered together in Christ, prefiguring the great day when the redeemed company would be drawn "from every nation, tribe, people and language" (Revelation 7:9).'

The catholic church must be equipped by the Holy Spirit in such a way that peoples of all the nations can hear 'the wonders of God in' their 'own tongues'. The church must be both local and international at the same time. On the birthday of the Christian church we catch a glimpse of 'the end in the middle': the prefiguring of the church at the end of time — which indeed must be too a church of all nations in the meantime.

It seems unlikely that this event was the first of many occasions throughout history that Christians have spoken in unintelligible tongues. Such occasions require an interpreter if *anybody* is going to hear *anything*. On this occasion *everybody* heard *something*, and therefore this occasion of Pentecost should not be confused with glossolalia or speaking in tongues.

Yet what this occasion underlines, is the place of experience in Christian discipleship. Christianity goes beyond the intellectual and conceptual, as it not only inflames the mind but also floods the heart and motivates the will. 'I will write my law in their inward hearts.' Such religious experience is nearly always expressed in body language. We see this at its fullest in the record of the Psalms. Tears, laughter, even belly-ache all have their place in the orchestration of religious experience. Furthermore, it often has confusing and overlapping manifestations: Hannah in the Old Testament was mistaken for being drunk, as the apostles in the New Testament were on the day of Pentecost. The one thing we can know for certain about religious experience is that things are not always what they seem to be.

Yet all these strange and embarrassing phenomena point to one reality. They are signs that the Holy Spirit is now in the driving seat rather than my rational, cautious and inhibited ego. The church cannot be equipped for its task of universal evangelism unless the Holy Spirit has taken over. Only so will we reverse the egotism of the Fall. Only so will men and women from all nations hear and receive the good news in their own language and in their own cultural experience. Babel in the Old Testament was the place and time when we tried to be God and 'wind ourselves' to heaven. Pentecost and Jerusalem in the New Testament are both the place and time when God the Holy Spirit humbly comes down to manage and organize his church for mission on earth. The mind, the ego and the personality all have their part to play in this drama so long as we allow another Author to write the script and the Holy Spirit to produce the performance. Christian disciples are men and women under orders.

Perhaps at the end of the day of Pentecost, they tore down the old sign outside the upper room: 'Peter, James and John, sons of Zebedee, Ltd' (very limited!) and in its place put up a new sign: 'Under new management'.

Experiencing Judgement

Now a man named Ananias, together with his wife Sapphira, also sold a piece of property. With his wife's full knowledge he kept back part of the money for himself, but brought the rest and put it at the apostles' feet.

Then Peter said, 'Ananias, how is it that Satan has so filled your heart that you have lied to the Holy Spirit and have kept for yourself some of the money you received for the land? Didn't it belong to you before it was sold? And after it was sold, wasn't the money at your disposal? What made you think of doing such a thing? You have not lied to men but to God.'

When Ananias heard this, he fell down and died. And great fear seized all who heard what had happened.

Acts 5:1—5

EVENT

Luke is an accurate and trustworthy historian. Many people today wish that this somewhat embarrassing account were not included in Luke's story of the rise of the early church. Yet Luke insists on giving it eleven verses to recount a rather sordid and dark event in the early life of the evolving church.

We need to recall, reaffirm again and again, that this side of the *parousia* the powers of light and darkness are still in combat and not least within the church. A true Pentecost will always be followed by persecution. A breakthrough for the armies of God will always mark the place and occasion of the subsequent and immediate counter-attack by Satan and his forces. So, as soon as chapter two of Acts concludes with its triumphant first evangelistic break-through and we see the church established in Jerusalem, Satan strategically moves in with a counter-attack on two fronts: fightings and persecutions without; broken fellowship and falsehood within. Luke refuses to tell only half the story. He tells all: the persecution of Peter and John, and now the deception and lies of Ananias and Sapphira. On both fronts the devil's aim is always the same: the destruction of the church, whether by external forces or internal divisions.

Many commentators see a direct parallel between Achan in the Old Testament and Ananias in the New Testament. Achan misappropriates property after God's people triumphantly enter into Jericho. So F.F. Bruce comments: 'The story of Ananias is to the book the Acts what the story of Achan is to the book of Joshua. In both narratives an act of deceit interrupts the victorious progress of the people of God.'

Notice that Peter is quite adamant. This is nothing less than the work of Satan (verse 3). Furthermore, the heart of this deception is a lie and a lie to God, at that.

EXPLANATION

'*On ne badine pas avec l'amour*' (You do not play about with love). Neither do you play about with the Holy Spirit. He is not a force of wind and fire one minute and the next minute a harmless sensation. The sin against the Holy Spirit to which Jesus refers in the gospel is a terrible reality with terrifying consequences both in this world and in the next world. A bad conscience always leads to dis-ease, though we must not make the mistake of reversing this truth: not all disease is directly attributable to sin or a bad conscience. A walking lie is a disfigured and deformed person. In the language of the Psalms, this is always experienced psychosomatically. We should not expect the gifts *from* the Holy Spirit to have a bodily expression (tears, laughter, tongues, etc.), while sins *against* the Holy Spirit remain innocuous and harmless. If you can rest in the Spirit, you can also be slain by the Spirit.

Christians are not duallists. There are not two gods, only One and he is Light. The devil is a fallen creature, and as such derives his strength, as all parasites, by battening on to the good. So he is at the arm of Jesus at the last supper, yet eventually he is expelled into the darkness outside the supper room, where he really belongs.

A church poised for renewal and evangelism should expect not only external destructive forces, but internal forces suddenly to break loose. The devil will not waste his time with a nice, cosy, harmless little congregation! When a church begins renewal, do not be surprised if at the outset, all hell is let loose!

Furthermore, we should not look for the perfect church. It does not exist; if it did, the moment I joined it, it would no longer be perfect! The church is a school for sinners, as well as a home for saints. Saints are repentant sinners — there is no other raw material with which to make a saint. But notice the need for repentance. Later in the story of Ananias, Peter deliberately gives his wife, Sapphira, the chance to tell the truth about the price of the land and therefore to repent.

A renewed church is the church most in need of church discipline and repentance. All sin divides the *koinonia* or fellowship of the Holy Spirit. Peter was not judgemental about Ananias and Sapphira. He himself had held back many times in his total commitment to Jesus and would do so again. Christians are sinners like anyone else. Yet when we 'fall into sin' we promise in our reaffirmation of our baptismal vows to 'repent and return to the Lord'.

'To turn aside from thee is hell;
To walk with thee is heaven.'

Confirmation in the Holy Spirit

When the apostles in Jerusalem heard that Samaria had accepted the word of God, they sent Peter and John to them. When they arrived, they prayed for them that they might receive the Holy Spirit, because the Holy Spirit had not yet come upon any of them; they had simply been baptised into the name of the Lord Jesus. Then Peter and John placed their hands on them, and they received the Holy Spirit.

Acts 8:14—17

EVENT

When Philip goes to proclaim Christ in Samaria, we reach another strategic turning point in Luke's record of the expanding church. 'Those who had been scattered' (by the persecution (verse 1)), 'preached the word wherever they went' — even in Samaria. Jesus had deliberately charged his disciples at his Ascension to include Samaria, but it is hard for us to realize what an enormously bold step Philip took when he proclaimed Christ in that no-go area — just as hard as it is for us to realize the full force of the story of the good Samaritan, also told to us only by St Luke in his gospel. The division between the Jew and the Samaritan went back a thousand years to the time when the ten tribes broke away and founded their own capital at Samaria. The situation deteriorated even further, when in the fourth century BC the Samaritans built their own temple at Mount Gerizim, and by the time of Jesus we read that Jews had no dealings whatever with Samaritans (John 4:9).

Now, Philip had broken down the 'Berlin Wall' and had preached the word of God effectively and with power even in Samaria. The news swiftly travelled back to Jerusalem and Peter and John were immediately sent to endorse and to confirm this new missionary breakthrough. When the two apostles arrived they were intent on receiving the new Christian Samaritans into the catholic fellowship of the church. There must be no continuation of the old schism, and certainly there must be no question of first class and second class Christians.

Yet Luke insists that the Samaritan Christians had not yet received the Holy Spirit and furthermore he insists that after the apostles laid their hands upon them they had received the Holy Spirit. It is worth noticing that Luke does not name a particular manifestation (tongues or prophecy) as the sign that these new Christians had or had not received the Holy Spirit.

EXPLANATION

Christians have been divided for a long time over this account in Acts. For some, this verse justifies a two-staged Christian initiation, while for others it would suggest that 'something went wrong' in the exceptional case of the baptism of these first Samaritan converts, for which Peter and John had, on this unique occasion, gone hot-foot to Samaria to rectify.

There is I believe a better explanation yet which is particularly applicable to our church in an age of renewal and fresh evangelism. Cyprian comments on this passage: 'Exactly the same thing happens with us today; those who have been baptised in the church are presented to the bishops of the church so that by our prayer and the imposition of our hands they may receive the Holy Spirit' (*Letters* 73:9). In the Prayer Book of 1662 and 1928 the bishop lays his hands upon the heads of the candidates and prays that they will daily increase in the Holy Spirit more and more. Baptism is both a once-for-all occasion and a continuing process. All the sacraments of the church are but an extension and extending of our once-for-all baptismal status.

After all, when does an acorn become an oak tree? When does a baptised Christian become a fully mature Christian? On the road of discipleship there are many road-blocks. The Christian life is the record of the Holy Spirit filling us ever more fully and breaking through first one and then another inhibition and road-block until it is no longer a question of how much of the Holy Spirit we have received, but rather of how much of us the Holy Spirit has possessed. Confirmation is a pastoral sacrament in our church and should be administered with bifocal lenses: it is both the occasion when new Christians are made and also when Christians are made new. So, thank God, Luke did not attach a particular sign (tongues, prophecy or anything else) to this further receiving of the Holy Spirit.

EXPERIENCE

Could it be that the Samaritan Christians were a particular example of a certain 'road-block'? After all, they were rather a special case. For so long they had been accustomed to being a schismatic party. Surely there was a real danger now, as Calvin says, that they might tear 'Christ apart' or form 'a new and separate church for themselves'. They needed confirmation in the unity of the Spirit. There could only be one body if there was one Spirit. Peter and John were sent by the apostolic college to receive them into that fuller fellowship of the one church and so to break down the road-block of schism or élitism which was inherent and already latent.

So when we evangelize in the Samarias of our day, there will be a particular danger of a tendency to speak of first and second class Christians. In the face of this we need to proclaim one baptism, one faith but also many applications of ministry to help to release people evermore fully into that one body and one Spirit — always refusing to name any one gift of the Spirit as being determinative of true and authentic discipleship. Rather we need to pray that both new Christians and renewed Christians alike may 'daily increase in his Holy Spirit more and more'.

Seeking the Wrong Experience

When Simon saw that the Spirit was given at the laying on of the apostles' hands, he offered them money and said, 'Give me also the ability so that everyone on whom I lay my hands may receive the Holy Spirit.'

Peter answered: 'May your money perish with you, because you thought you could buy the gift of God with money! You have no part or share in this ministry, because your heart is not right before God. Repent of this wickedness and pray to the Lord. Perhaps he will forgive you for having such a thought in your heart. For I see that you are full of bitterness and captive to sin.'

The Simon answered, 'Pray to the Lord for me so that nothing you have said may happen to me.'

When they had testified and proclaimed the word of the Lord, Peter and John returned to Jerusalem, preaching the gospel in many Samaritan villages.

Acts 8:18—25

EVENT

Simon was a man of considerable spiritual power and had many spiritual gifts. He was not a bad man and there was a lot of good in him. People were amazed by his magic arts and crafts and clearly he had great influence in Samaria. People were *amazed* by Simon, but Luke goes on to tell us that they *believed* Philip and his message — there was the difference! Simon also believed Philip. He was baptised and then 'followed Philip everywhere, astonished by the great signs and miracles he saw'.

When Simon observed the great power that the apostles wielded in their ministry, he wanted to have just that same power for himself. He supposed that he could buy this power and hence he has given his name throughout history to the practice and abuse of seeking to buy high office in the church — Simony. It is bad enough to be materialistic, but to be materialistic about spiritual things verges on the demonic. That was precisely the substance of the devil's temptation of Jesus in the wilderness. The perversion of spiritual power is a terrible thing.

So Peter calls upon Simon to repent and to change his whole attitude to power and to spiritual gifts. Simon wanted the gifts without the Giver, so that he could remain in control and manipulate people with his considerable spiritual gifts and with the power he saw exercised at the hands of the apostles.

EXPLANATION

'Unusual physiological or psychic powers appear to be innate human capacities that can be developed by practising certain disciplines,' writes Thomas Keating, a contemporary master of the spiritual life. 'But they have nothing to do with holiness or the growth of our relationship to God. To regard them as a sign of great spiritual development is a mistake.'

We live at a time when two phenomena are very apparent: a dramatic increase in religion outside the church: spiritual craving, superstition, magic and the demonic. Also within the church there is a spectacular revival of the traditional gifts of the Spirit such as speaking in tongues, singing in tongues, resting in the Spirit, healing, prophecy and the like.

In the first place, the fact that our western world has flipped from a jaundiced materialism to a mindless spiritualism does not represent a step forward. The devil can gain access to a mindless spiritualism more easily than he can to a blatant materialism. He likes to masquerade as spiritual and he certainly has his charismatics.

Secondly, a revival in the church of interest in the spiritual life, needs to be matched with a genuine repentance and at the same time calls for a new need for that precious ministry of discernment of which John wrote. Peter was exercising the apostolic gift of discernment when he saw that Simon wished to abuse and prostitute spiritual powers.

In the New Testament we are given a double command: 'Resist not the Spirit', yet at the same time, 'Test the spirits.' 'By their fruits you shall know them,' says Jesus and the first fruit of the Holy Spirit is supremely the fruit of love — yet love as defined for us by St Paul in 1 Corinthians 13, and supremely as we see it in the life of Jesus. So Paul can write — 'Though I speak with the tongues of men and of angels', and have all the spiritual gifts but have not love, I am nothing.

We must give thanks to God for the great spiritual awakening which is sweeping through all the churches today and to which we give the umbrella name of 'renewal'. But at the same time we must recognize the dangers of an obsession with and a covetousness of gifts rather than the worship of the Giver. It is holiness of life we must seek, pointing as it does not to self and to gifts however spectacular, but rather consistently pointing to the Giver of all the gifts including the most important of all — love. The truly spiritual person is one who is totally unselfconscious, is caught up in trying to express the love of God which has taken hold of every aspect of their life — a life spent in love and service for others. 'True religion,' insists St James, is not the exercising of spectacular, impressive, spiritual powers, but rather something as down to earth as looking 'after orphans and widows in their distress' and keeping oneself unpolluted from the materialism of the world (James 1:27).

A Converting Experience

Meanwhile, Saul was still breathing out murderous threats against the Lord's disciples. He went to the high priest and asked him for letters to the synagogues in Damascus, so that if he found any there who belonged to the Way, whether men or women, he might take them as prisoners to Jerusalem. As he neared Damascus on his journey, suddenly a light from heaven flashed around him. He fell to the ground and heard a voice say to him, 'Saul, Saul, why do you persecute me?'

'Who are you, Lord?' Saul asked.

'I am Jesus, whom you are persecuting,' he replied. 'Now get up and go into the city, and you will be told what you must do.'

The men travelling with Saul stood there speechless; they heard the sound but did not see anyone. Saul got up from the ground, but when he opened his eyes he could see nothing. So they led him by the hand into Damascus. For three days he was blind, and did not eat or drink anything.

Acts 9:1—9

EVENT

The story of Paul's conversion on the road to Damascus occurs three times in the book of Acts: once in the course of the narrative (chapter 9) and twice more on the lips of Paul when he was called upon to witness to his faith (22:6ff and 26:12ff). Obviously there are two kinds of ingredients in the story. Some ingredients are peculiar to Paul's particular conversion while other elements are strangely common to all Christian conversions. We need to look at both.

Paul had been wrestling aggressively with the whole issue of Christianity and the resurrection of Jesus. Luke sows the seed of the inner battle of Saul of Tarsus in chapters seven and eight (at Stephen's martyrdom) and again when we were told of Saul's determination to destroy the church (8:3). Conversions are seldom a bolt from the blue: rather they are the tip of the iceberg. The contemporary proverb which was common in both Latin and Greek sayings of the first century, suggests that Saul had been kicking against the goads (26:14). Goads were used to break in a wild and ferocious bullock. Paul had heard a great deal about Jesus second-hand; we have no evidence of a first-hand encounter before the ascension of Jesus. Stephen had witnessed most dramatically to the risen Christ in his dying words, which were probably still ringing in Saul's ears. And now as though 'methinks he protested too much', here he is, hell-bent on the hundred-and-forty mile journey on foot from Jerusalem to Damascus with letters of extradition from the high priest. Yet his mind was wrestling with doubts — those kind of doubts which are what Frederick Beaconer so strikingly describes as 'the ants in the pants of faith'! Then as Paul draws near to Damascus, suddenly he is struck, as by lightning. In his own description of the experience he uses a verb in Greek which suggests that he was 'arrested'. Ironically, Christ arrested him (Philippians 3:12) when he was on his way to arrest others, not unlike Peter being hooked and caught by Jesus when he was on his way to catch and hook the fishes. Saul was blinded by light and fell to the ground. From all the three records, Saul asks two fundamental questions: 'Who are you Lord?' and 'What am I to do?'

EXPLANATION

'You did not choose me, but I chose you,' says Jesus (John 15:16). Saul was not looking for Jesus; he was hiding from him, beneath frenetic, religious activity. In the game of hide-and-seek, it is not we who are looking for God: rather we are like Adam, afraid and we hide ourselves — often behind religion! Yet, the Son of Man came to seek and to save' (Luke 19:10). So the hound of heaven persists and pursues. C.S. Lewis likens God's pursuit of him, to 'the great Angler playing his fish, to a cat chasing a mouse . . . and finally to the divine chess player manoevring him into the disadvantageous positions until in the end he concedes "checkmate"' (*Surprised by Joy*).

Yet although the Damascus road represents a once-for-all turning point of conversion, nevertheless conversion is also a continuous process of sanctification and total surrender. In Philippians, a letter written much later in Paul's life, Paul tells us that he has still not completely made either Christianity or Jesus Christ his own, but rather presses on to take hold of him who first took hold of Paul on that Damascus road (Philippians 3:12f).

EXPERIENCE

Yet in a real sense, Saul was converted at a place and at a point in time. 'You will be told what to do.' From now onwards, Paul is no longer his own man: he is Christ's man. Always accustomed to going where he wanted, he is now to go where he is told to go! Accustomed to doing his own will, he will now do what he is told to do. Damascus was only one more step, yet it was the decisive step from which all else followed.

We must preach and witness in season and out of season, for we never know who is listening or looking in the crowd. We do not need to brainwash or manipulate. God is already at work as the hound of heaven. The two questions which the world outside is asking are very much the questions on Saul's lips: 'Who on earth is Jesus?' and 'What on earth am I supposed to be doing with my life?' And in many ways those who are nearest to the kingdom by approach are often those who protest loudest and longest against the true answers to those questions. To be passionately wrong is often better than to be apathetically neutral.

Experiencing a Change of Heart

About noon the following day as they were on their journey and approaching the city, Peter went up on the roof to pray. He became hungry and wanted something to eat, and while the meal was being prepared, he fell into a trance. He saw heaven opened and something like a large sheet being let down to earth by its four corners. It contained all kinds of four-footed animals, as well as reptiles of the earth and birds of the air. Then a voice told him, 'Get up, Peter. Kill and eat.'

'Surely not, Lord!' Peter replied. 'I have never eaten anything impure or unclean.'

The voice spoke to him a second time, 'Do not call anything impure that God has made clean.'

This happened three times, and immediately the sheet was taken back to heaven.

Acts 10:9—16

EVENT

We have reached another road-block on the road of the church's mission from Jerusalem to the ends of the earth. Peter had been brought up not only to have no dealings with Samaritans, but of course to have no religious dealings whatever with Gentiles. Around Judaism, the Old Testament had drawn all kinds of lines and distinctions. One of the most distinctive lines was the line between Jew and Gentile. It was hard to believe now that the apostles at the outset of their ministry truly believed that their faith in Jesus Christ was to be shared only with Jews or if not, then at least with Gentiles who kept the whole ritual law of circumcision and the food laws as recorded in the book of Leviticus. The devout Jew, generally speaking, could eat only those animals which chewed the cud and whose hooves were cloven. All other animals were regarded as unclean and therefore were forbidden as food for the devout Jew.

There is some suggestion in this story that Peter had already begun to see beyond the line, to see through all of this. Luke tells us that he was 'staying with Simon the tanner', whose house 'was by the sea' (9:43, 10:6). Obviously a tanner would have to work with the dead bodies of animals and therefore, according to the Old Testament, he would be perpetually 'unclean' (Numbers 19:11–13). No orthodox Jew would have accepted hospitality from such a person. It was this kind of ritual uncleanness which would demand that Simon the tanner lived outside the city. If he was a Christian, then perhaps Peter was already turning over in his mind the relationship between Christianity and the rules and laws of the Old Testament. After all Jesus Christ had died outside the city for the marginalized, the outcast and the outsider.

In any event, Peter went on to the roof-top to pray. From there he would be able to see the sailing ships passing by on the Mediterranean with their huge sails. Furthermore, we are told that he was hungry and that the smell of food being prepared below might well have been wafting up to the roof-tops as Peter fell into his sleep or trance.

EXPLANATION

Two elements of the world around Peter passed into the world within him. The sheet in the trance is in fact a sailcloth and the substance of the trance is connected with appetite, eating food. Two if not three of the senses are involved in the trance: sight, taste and possibly smell.

That is the way we experience God within us. We never have a purely ethereal, neat spiritual experience: that is for angels! God always uses the here-and-now to point us to the there-and-then. There is a connection between the world around us and the world within us. Dreams are frequently the occasions where that connection is made. For Christianity is not a spiritual religion: it is essentially a sacramental faith in which the outward and visible acts as the vehicle for the inward and spiritual.

So, in that trance, God draws a line right through the cautious lines of the Jewish law. 'Do not call anything impure that God has made clean.' Little wonder that this left Peter wondering: he had to unlearn everything he had ever learnt as a devout Jew. In a word, he had to have second thoughts and the word for that in the New Testament is that keyword for all Christians — repent.

EXPERIENCE

'Where there is no vision the people perish' (Proverbs 29:18). Christians must learn to live in the school of the Holy Spirit — to make the connection between accidents and providence; between the outward and visible and the inward and the spiritual; between the here-and-now and the there-and-then. All of life for a Christian is a sacrament, for those with eyes to see and ears to hear.

And wherever we draw a line we can be sure that God will always draw another line right through it. It is of course the sign of the cross — the sign of unconditional love which goes beyond time and space. There is no 'apartheid' in Christian mission and evangelism.

Finally, if we are to experience the work of the Holy Spirit to bring about that change of heart which is so necessary on the road to salvation, reconciliation and healing, then we must always retain the capacity to wonder greatly, to be amazed, surprised and perplexed. That was Peter's experience: we read that he was 'inwardly perplexed' (RSV). Yet such is the prelude to true repentance. For on second thoughts, when we begin to see things from a new perspective and a different point of view, we are in fact repenting.

The church throughout its history has drawn all kinds of lines and oppressed the faith with petty rules and taboos. The lines of class, of colour, of race, of family and gender have fragmented the body of Christ and drained our energies. We need to repent of our past. For in Christ's church 'there is neither Greek nor Jew, bond nor free, male nor female', the apostle to the Gentiles reminds us.

An Assuring Experience

Then Paul left the synagogue and went next door to the house of Titius Justus, a worshipper of God. Crispus, the synagogue ruler, and his entire household believed in the Lord; and many of the Corinthians who heard him believed and were baptised.

One night the Lord spoke to Paul in a vision: 'Do not be afraid; keep on speaking, do not be silent. For I am with you, and no one is going to attack and harm you, because I have many people in this city.' So Paul stayed for a year and a half, teaching them the word of God.

Acts 18:7—11

EVENT

In AD 49/50 Paul came from Athens to Corinth for the first time. He had just come from his Mars Hill encounter in Athens, where he took a philosophical approach to Christianity. Paul's mission to Athens met with little success and he did not found a church there. Later Paul says of this visit to Corinth: 'I came to you in weakness and fear and with much trembling.' Furthermore he tells us that he resolved when going to Corinth from Athens 'to know nothing' while he was in Corinth, 'except Jesus Christ and him crucified' (1 Corinthians 2:2). Going from Athens to Corinth would be like going from Princeton to Los Angeles or Oxford to Liverpool. Yet Paul had learned his lesson. There was power in the word of the cross. Neither in Athens nor in Corinth would 'clever' words bring men and women to a saving knowledge of Christ.

Corinth was a proud and immoral city. Corinthians had a great pride in their splendid city, beautifully rebuilt in 46 BC as a strategic port and trading centre between the Adriatic and the Aegean. Behind the ancient port city, you can still see Acrocorinth at two thousand feet above sea level. There stood the temple of Aphrodite — the goddess of love. 'Corinthian' was a byword in the ancient world for immorality, and was almost a synonym for prostitute. For Corinth was the Las Vegas and Bangkok of the ancient world. Yet it was here that Paul was to found one of the most alive and robust churches of his whole missionary strategy.

At first, on his arrival he pursued his trade as a tentmaker. Tarsus of Cilicia, the home of Paul, was noted for a coarse fabric made from the thick, local goats' hair, called in Latin *cilicium*. Paul, as a rabbi, would be compelled to have a trade as well as his profession and calling as a rabbi. 'Love work,' said the Jewish tradition. 'He who does not teach his son a trade, teaches him robbery.' 'Excellent is the study of the law along with a wordly trade; for the practice of them both makes a man forget iniquity.' So Paul is not ashamed to pursue his trade.

But then, Silas and Timothy arrive (verse 5), bringing with them a present (probably from Philippi where Paul was greatly loved). At last Paul is set free from the need to earn money and is able to devote himself 'exclusively to preaching'.

EXPLANATION

Paul is strengthened for his evangelistic task by the companionship of Aquila and Priscilla, who had been expelled from Rome and who had arrived very conveniently at Corinth. Also, Silas and Timothy were now his companions in the gospel. 'There are no lone-rangers in the kingdom,' Peter Wagner would remind us.

It would seem that after Athens and on his arrival in Corinth, Paul lost his nerve a little. So there is a word from the Lord for him to comfort, encourage and goad him in his missionary endeavours.

In a vision in the night, Paul receives a comfortable word.

'Do not be afraid.' Often in the New Testament when someone is being called to new responsibilities and particular ministry for the kingdom, they receive this word from God: 'Do not be afraid.'

'Go on speaking', in season and out of season and be assured that I am with you, says the Lord. This same Lord Jesus has gone ahead of Paul in his missionary journeys and has already prepared the hearts of 'many people' in the city of Corinth to hear and receive the word of God.

Paul is set free from financial anxieties and from loneliness and fear to spend the next eighteen months in Corinth — of all places — where there was to be a rich harvest.

EXPERIENCE

The church is often strongest in the last place on earth we would ever expect God's word to flourish. It is the alcoholic, the drug-addicted, the erotomaniac, the prisoner and the outcast who most know their need of God (Matthew 5:3 NEB). The self-sufficient, the smug and the clever are often more difficult to evangelize. No wonder Paul says that there are not many upper class, not 'many wise by human standards; not many . . . influential, not many . . . of noble birth' listed among the members of the church in Corinth.

'Whom he calls he empowers,' says St Anselm. St Paul was not a very large and impressive man according to Eusebius, the fourth-century historian. He could not speak very well. We do not need to be clever, impressive or eloquent to evangelize. Our strength is in the Lord and in the knowledge that he is with us at all times — not to take us out of the crisis, the dangers and the difficulties, but to be with us *in* the crisis and to bring us through it. We do not need to know the details of the harvest. He is Lord of the harvest. Our task is to go on casting the seed whether the ground looks promising or not. Often the most fertile ground is where you would least expect to find it.

At his baptism, Jesus was anointed with the Holy Spirit. Then in the next verse we read: 'At once the Spirit sent him out into the desert' (Mark 1:12). The word used in Greek for sending him out is a powerful compound word — *ekballō*— giving us our word ballistic missile. Jesus was baptised for mission and the Holy Spirit was given to expel Jesus into the 'god-forsaken' area of the desert for confrontation with evil.

Whenever we pray for a fresh anointing of the Holy Spirit, we had better look out! Because that is where he will send us — out, to the most unpromising places, to confront evil by word and deed and to proclaim the coming of the kingdom to the last place on earth we would ever expect it to come.

We speak today of the renewal of the church with a new sense of Pentecost, a new expectation of God the Holy Spirit. But we must remember that we are rescued from sin and death for renewal in mission and evangelism. Any evangelization will inevitably bring us into direct conflict with the kingdoms of this world and the kingdom of the devil. Renewal and the giving of the Spirit are not a cosy and comfortable experience to be enjoyed by anybody in a secluded upper room. It expels and explodes them from that upper room into ministry and mission. The story of the Transfiguration tells us that the disciples were overshadowed afresh by the cloud of the Holy Spirit on that mountain-top, with a transfiguring experience of the real presence of Jesus in all his majesty and in communion with his saints — holy Moses and holy Elijah. But almost 'at once' (one of Mark's favourite phrases), that same Holy Spirit expelled them from the mountain of the transfiguration down to the valley below, for confrontation with evil, disease and sickness. The Holy Spirit is given to be given away in mission, compassion and to be spent in confrontation with evil. When the worship is over the service begins — or it could also be translated: when the mass is ended the mission begins.

Jesus was baptised with the Holy Spirit for mission, and so are we. Notice how he refutes the evil one in the desert. The Holy Spirit brings to his mind the words of scripture — three times, like claps of thunder: 'it is written . . . it is written . . . it is written.'

The Holy Spirit, Jesus assures us, will do the same thing for us. He will take the words of Jesus and bring them to our remembrance. Furthermore the very words we speak in Spirit-driven mission will be anointed and powerful to refute lies and to confront evil.

Notice also the place where the church is expelled to for mission — to those god-forsaken areas of the world. Jesus deliberately lists Samaria in the list of missionary map-references — when he is outlining the course of mission to the disciples before his Ascension. That was certainly the last place in the world a Jew would ever expect to go on mission.

Because, you see, in the Old Testament way of seeing things, a Jew did not think of world mission as explosion at all. Rather, it was for him and even for the most enlightened Jew of the old Israel, essentially a matter of implosion not explosion. Mission in the Old Testament was primarily a 'pilgrimage of the nations' to Mount Zion: Isaiah forsees and foretells 'all nations' streaming to Mount Zion (Isaiah 2:2—3). Johannes Blauw, in his book, *The Missionary Nature of the Church*, says only in the new Israel is a 'centripetal missionary consciousness' replaced by a 'centrifugal missionary activity'. Mohammed was supposed to go to the mountain, but in the New Testament the mountain must be moved to go to Mohammed.

And all that is because of the great explosion at the heart of God himself. Since the beginning of time God has been sending people on his errands — and everybody from Abraham to Jeremiah was sent. In these last days, he has sent his Son. Love goes out of its way — it always does. And perhaps that is the best definition of mission and evangelism. Love has gone out of its way and the church is caught up in that explosion of love. God 'so loved the world . . .

that he sent.' That is the motivation and direction of mission, exploding outwards from the heart of God and of heaven itself to the ends of the earth. The Holy Spirit was given for ballistic mission, 'until the earth is filled with the glory of God, as the waters cover the sea'.

Questions for reflection during the week and for discussion in the group

1. If renewal leads to new mission responsibilities, has it done so for me and for the local congregation where I worship?
2. What is the most god-forsaken area of my life, my community and in our nation today? Am I prepared (by the Holy Spirit) to see that these areas are addressed with the anointed word of God?
3. How do I 'read, mark, learn and inwardly digest' the scriptures? Could I recall a verse or passage as a comfortable word at any time of the day or night? Are there any Bible study groups in my parish: if not, is it time for me to start one?
4. When did I last talk about my life with a relative or a close friend and share my story of faith with someone else — possibly one who does not go to church?

Explosive Prayer

On their release, Peter and John went back to their own people and reported all that the chief priests and elders had said to them. When they heard this, they raised their voices together in prayer to God. 'Sovereign Lord,' they said, 'you made the heaven and the earth and the sea, and everything in them. You spoke by the Holy Spirit through the mouth of your servant, our father David:

"Why do the nations rage,

and the peoples plot in vain? . . ."
Indeed Herod and Pontius Pilate met together with the Gentiles and the people of Israel in this city to conspire against your holy servant Jesus, whom you anointed. They did what your power and will had decided beforehand should happen. Now, Lord, consider their threats and enable your servants to speak your word with great boldness. Stretch out your hand to heal and perform miraculous signs and wonders through the name of your holy servant Jesus.'

After they prayed, the place where they were meeting was shaken. And they were all filled with the Holy Spirit and spoke the word of God boldly.

Acts 4:23—25, 27—31

EVENT

Notice the rhythm of this passage and therefore the rhythm in the apostolic life of the early church. The apostles move from witness to prayer and back again from prayer to witness. Having witnessed before the Council to Jesus, they returned to the Lord in prayer. Having prayed, they are then strengthened again for faithful witness; being filled afresh with the Holy Spirit, they return to the outside world and speak 'the word of God boldly'. Witness retreats into worship and in turn worship inevitably explodes back into witness. 'When the worship is ended the service begins.'

What kind of prayer is it then which will empower the church to go out and witness boldly? What sort of prayer is it which empowers the church to be truly apostolic?

'Sovereign Lord,' they begin. The word in Greek is *despotēs* — despot. It is a term used for the owner of slaves and for one whose power is infinite. 'He's got the whole world in his hands,' we sing. But do we believe it? Those first apostles clearly did.

They recovered their nerve by remembering and recalling his power. This God of theirs is a God who has *created* everything (verse 24). He has spoken and *revealed* himself through his servants

---

(25). He has *anointed* and *empowered* Jesus, his 'holy servant' (27). This God has shown himself to be creator, redeemer and sanctifier in the past — there and then. What is stopping him from doing all this here and now? That is the theme and confidence of their prayer.

'Dependence upon him, upon whom all things depend,' says Tillich. Or as St Paul says: 'For no one can lay any foundation other than the one already laid, which is Jesus Christ' (1 Corinthians 3:11). Jesus Christ is the foundation of all effective prayer, which is why all prayer is in and 'through Jesus Christ our Lord'. So, 'stretch out your hand to heal and perform miraculous signs and wonders through the name of your holy servant Jesus,' is their earnest petition. They pray for healing in this terrible situation of the tyranny of Herod and Pilate and they believe that good will come out of this evil. That prayer was answered powerfully and with particularity. Have you made the connection and followed up to see where and when that prayer was answered? (Do you keep a spiritual journal and a record of prayers made and prayers answered?) Luke tells us only eight chapters later that Herod died an untimely and sudden death; history tells us that Pilate lost his job and was banished to another part of the empire. But 'the word of God continued to increase and spread': that is the last word on this whole chapter of expansion and persecution (12:24).

Expectant prayer in the power of the Spirit, recalling and remembering the mighty acts of God in the past, is the explosive prayer of the present. And it is the kind of prayer on which the apostolic church was built.

Notice that the foundations of the building in which the church met were 'shaken'. The church is founded upon Jesus Christ, and that

---

foundation cannot be shaken. So often throughout history the church has relied upon earthly powers, political power and financial power, and it has built its foundation upon them. Equally often in history that church has fallen into dust and ruins. For the church that is built on the quicksands of earthly power will always fall when the testing storms of persecution come and it will fall 'with a great crash' (Matthew 7:27 NIV).

Faith and prayer in Jesus Christ constitute the rock on which he has built his church and the gates of hell cannot prevail against it. Herod and Pilate, Stalin and Amin have all had their 'little day', but the apostolic church of Jesus Christ is still standing and always will — as long as it remains a praying church relying upon the foundations of faith; filled with the Holy Spirit and speaking the word of God boldly.

Martin Luther was warned of the disasterous results of persisting in his faith. 'In the end, all your supporters will desert you,' he was warned. 'Where will you be then?' he was asked. 'Then as now,' he replied, 'in the hands of God.'

Only a church which attempts the impossible will prove the power of prayer and the words of Jesus are painfully and joyfully all too true: 'Apart from me you can do nothing' (John 15:5).

Inside Out

All the believers were one in heart and mind. No one claimed that any of his possessions was his own, but they shared everything they had. With great power the apostles continued to testify to the resurrection of the Lord Jesus, and much grace was upon them all.

There were no needy persons among them. For from time to time those who owned lands or houses sold them, brought the money from the sales and put it at the apostles' feet, and it was distributed to anyone as he had need.

Acts 4:32—35

Luke has continuity in all his basic themes. The great basic theme throughout the book of Acts is the constant witness and testimony to the resurrection of Jesus. 'Jesus and the resurrection': that was their story and that was their song.

Yet actions speak louder than words. It takes more than just words and talk to convince and convert people. People are impressed by apostolic eloquence but they are even more impressed by apostolic deeds. It was not simply a question of the way those early Christians talked that was so moving and impressive. It was much more a question of the way they lived.

'No one claimed that any of his possessions were his own.' That is a most revolutionary statement. Furthermore, it made a statement in a language which was common currency and evident for all to see. It was not just paying lip-service to the reality of Jesus and the resurrection: it showed in their lifestyle.

In the past, in the world at large, it had been every man for himself. Suddenly, now it was man for others. The power of the resurrection and the Holy Spirit at work in their lives had suddenly turned their lives inside out.

We need to notice two results. 'They were one in heart and mind.' Unity was no longer just an idea or an ideal. Their faith affected and infected not only their minds, but their hearts and wills. What previously had divided them (class divisions and wealth) now united them. The barrier of language fell at Pentecost but the barriers of property fell daily as they witnessed to the lordship of Jesus. In a word, they were living the common life of the body of Christ.

Secondly, instead of worshipping money, they were bringing

their money under the lordship of Christ — placing it, literally, at the feet of the apostles. Money is there to be used and managed, whether there is a lot of it or little of it. When it manages us and takes over our lives, then we have fallen into materialism.

EXPLANATION

Christianity is not a spiritual religion. It is a sacramental faith. When we begin to live the life of Christ, it shows up on every front and changes the profile of history. Money, sex, ambition, drink — all these have been at the root of divisions, strife and isolation. But they do not disappear in the spiritual life; they simply cease to rule us. They must be brought to the feet of Christ and be subject to his most gracious reign. Jesus is Lord, and God has put all things under his feet. So we are set free from their bondage and we are raised up by Jesus our Lord to be stewards of the universe, re-ordering the world and placing it at the disposal of Christ our King. Then, and only then, will evolution cease to be the law of the jungle, the survival of the fittest and a question of every man for himself. It will then be a case of man for others, each for the other because all are for Jesus and Jesus is all for God!

EXPERIENCE

For we were not born to live for ourselves. That is not life but death. We were born to be possessed. The hole in all our hearts will be filled sooner or later with something. Like the rich young ruler, we could end up being possessed by our possessions.

So there is only one way through the jungle of possessions: surrender. If we worship the creation and are possessed by our possessions, we are slaves. They are all false gods, leading their worshippers into slavery and bondage. The alcoholic does not even enjoy drink and the gambler is notoriously, perpetually bored. We were made to worship God and 'enjoy him for ever'. The opposite of sin is not virtue. The opposite of sin is true worship: bringing everything, 'ourselves, our souls and bodies', to the altar of the Lord. Then and only then will our will be turned inside out and we shall be of one heart and mind, because we have one faith and *worship* one Lord. That is true unity of heart and mind. The common life is the most powerful witness to the Lordship of Christ and therefore to the truth of the resurrection.

All the good things in life destroy and divide us if we mistake them for the best, put them in the place of God and begin to fall down at *their* feet and worship them. The enemy of the best is not only the worst; it is also the good — good but not good enough to satisfy us for ever.

So often we try to *get round* this competitive market, by pretending that all these things are bad: money, sex, ambition, greed, etc. That is puritanism and it is not the answer. We need rather to recognize all these good gifts of God for what they are: *neither more nor less*. There is no need to *get round* this competitive market, but rather the way through is by the common market of true religion, where there is no distinction of class, colour or race. No one claims anything is their own because all things are ours. Yet only all things are ours if we are first the property of Christ, and Christ is God's own and richest gift to the whole world. Only the kingdom of God in the end is the true common market, because in the end only he is king and all things are brought in subjection under his feet.

An Inside Job?

Then the high priest and all his associates, who were members of the party of the Sadducees, were filled with jealousy. They arrested the apostles and put them in the public jail. But during the night an angel of the Lord opened the doors of the jail and brought them out. 'Go, stand in the temple courts,' he said, 'and tell the people the full message of this new life.'

At daybreak they entered the temple courts, as they had been told, and began to teach the people.

Acts 5:17—21

EVENT

The most fierce opposition to the living faith of Christianity has always been religion. It was the religious people who were most opposed to Jesus — the Pharisees and the Sadducees.

The Sadducees were particularly opposed to Jesus. They were the priestly aristocracy; they ran the temple and they organized the Jewish religion. We know from the New Testament, as well as from elsewhere, that they did not believe in the resurrection or the supernatural (Acts 23:8). Their mind-set was closed to any surprises in the universe: they had their religion all cut and dried. They believed in religion and organized religion at that.

Everything about the apostles and their message constituted a threat to that closed system — especially the healing of the sick. The Sadducees coveted control and clearly they could not control or manage the kind of power that was being exercised by the apostles before their very eyes and before the eyes of half the population of Jerusalem.

So they would do with the apostles and the new life which they exemplified what they had already done with the faith of Judaism. They would lock it up and imprison it so that it could not get out of control — namely, their control.

EXPLANATION

William Neil in his commentary on the book of Acts is determined to write out anything supernatural about the angel deliverer in Luke's account and insists that the angel was just 'a sympathetic warder or a secret sympathiser' among the guard-room and the staff of the prison — an 'angel' yes, but an angel in disguise as he would prefer us to say. In other words he wants to re-write this whole event as 'an inside job'.

But it will not do. The angel does not only let them out, but sends them out under orders: telling them where to go and what to say.

For truth to tell, man's salvation and deliverance is essentially and necessarily not an *inside job*. God 'so loved the world that he sent' from the outside the message and the messenger to open the door of our prison house, and release the captives — and not least to release all who had been imprisoned by that most subtle captivity: the captivity of religion. For William Neil was not a liberal in his thought. On the contrary, he was under the bondage of the religion of his mind where the intellect rules supreme. He needed liberating from the tyranny of the mind — and that was not an inside job. He needed, as we all do, more than just an educator: he needed a saviour and deliverer.

There have always been those throughout history who want to re-write and reduce Christianity to a system of rules and therefore to a religion. Christianity is not a system, a religion or a set of rules: Christianity is not any *thing*. Christianity is some*body*: it is Jesus and the resurrection. It is faith in an empty tomb with the stone rolled back and the captive of death released into the fuller environment of new life.

EXPERIENCE

And in the end, that is the choice. Is Christianity a man-made religion or a God-given faith: an inside job or essentially the work of the One who is beyond and outside? For orthodox Christianity has always insisted that he came from the outside to be inside — we call it the incarnation. He came to set us free and in turn to send us back out into the world to proclaim by word and deed 'the full message of this new life'.

For the new life has broken loose from the bonds of religion, the grave and the prison life — the intellect and the self. 'It is for freedom that Christ has set us free' (Galatians 5:1).

'Jesus came to save us from religion,' says Paul Tillich. We need to remember, however, that we are freed in order to set others free. We are healed in order to heal others and the door of our prison house has been opened so that we in turn may go out and open the doors of the hearts of others. Easter joy must lead to Pentecost mission.

What a pity that when the officers of the Sanhedrin arrived at the prison and found it empty they were blind to the full significance of this miraculous deliverance. Unlike 'the other disciple' in St John's gospel, when the evidence was staring them in the face, they were unable to 'see and believe'. We all have the same evidence but many are blinded to its significance. The minds of those officers were closed and locked; there was no longer any room left in their universe for resurrection, surprise or the supernatural. Yet only an outside job can open those doors of perception. Perhaps, like William Neil, the Sadducees were the captives of their own mind-set. Are we?

God's Agents

So Peter was kept in prison, but the church was earnestly praying to God for him.

The night before Herod was to bring him to trial, Peter was sleeping between two soldiers, bound with two chains, and sentries stood guard at the entrance. Suddenly an angel of the Lord appeared and a light shone in the cell. He struck Peter on the side and woke him up. 'Quick, get up!' he said, and the chains fell off Peter's wrists.

Then the angel said to him, 'Put on your clothes and sandals.' And Peter did so. 'Wrap your cloak around you and follow me,' the angel told him. Peter followed him out of the prison, but he had no idea that what the angel was doing was really happening; he though he was seeing a vision. They passed the first and second guards and came to the iron gate leading to the city. It opened for them by itself, and they went through it. When they had walked the length of one street, suddenly the angel left him.

Then Peter came to himself and said, 'Now I know without a doubt that the Lord sent his angel and rescued me from Herod's clutches and from everything the Jewish people were anticipating.'

Acts 12:5–11

EVENT

Who are all the active participants in his drama of release? There are three: the praying church; the obedient and perplexed Peter; and the angel. If God's will is to be done, on earth as in heaven, all three participants are needed.

First there is a praying and expectant church which is ready to 'hope all things' (1 Corinthians 13:7). Secondly there is Peter, a man under orders. The angel tells him in precise detail what he must do. Peter does as he is told, not necessarily understanding everything as he is doing it. It only 'dawns' on him later when the full significance of his actions becomes evident (verses 11–12).

The angel is the third character in the drama. The angel is the messenger between two worlds, seeking to do the will of God across the frontier. The angels are those supernatural agencies who can walk through all the doors between all the worlds — those doors that divide the inside from the outside, earth from heaven. The problems of the world are more than natural problems and they demand more than natural solutions. And all three participants are necessary for the fulfilment of God's will. That will is nothing less than the salvation of the whole world.

We do not pray in order to twist God's arm and persuade him to do what he does not want to do. Rather, we bring our hearts, lives and wills into line with what God wants to do, but what he has chosen to do only with our co-operation. God created the world by a divine *fiat*. 'Let there be light,' he said, and there was light. Not so, however with redemption. God could have redeemed us equally with a similar divine *fiat*. However, he has chosen not to do so. Redemption involves our co-operation through the re-orientation of our wills, our hearts, our minds and our energies. That re-orientation is expressed through work and prayer, together with the mission of the angels. 'It is impossible to pray sincerely for the well being of others, without being desirous of contributing to it' (Hannah More, *The Spirit of Prayer*). There is no such thing as purely spiritual prayer: prayer and work belong together. When all of our energies converge with the will of God, then mountains are easy to move and prison doors simply fall open. What we choose to call supernatural or miraculous then begins to fall within the realm of the probable and the purely natural.

However, please note that we do not need to understand God's will before we can begin to do it. Often it is in the doing of his will that we begin to see and understand his purpose. God generally makes his will clear to us, retrospectively, when we can see his hand in events. At the time, however, we often think we are dreaming.

Finally it is difficult to over-estimate the place in our everyday lives of what we like to call the supernatural. How, if we are open to the supernatural invasion of the natural, by the angelic host, then all things are possible. However, we must be obedient and welcome that dimension of grace into our lives, as Mary did when she was visited by the angel Gabriel. In a word, we must like her and together with her learn to say the simple Yes, amen, *fiat mihi* (let it be to me), of loving obedience. We must let the Spirit have his way with us as she did with her consent, to lead us in the right way — the way which leads from darkness to light, from bondage to freedom, from death to life.

Both before and after any great enterprise for God we must always recruit a whole army of intercessors and pray-ers. 'Pray-ers and players' have an equally important part in God's drama for the salvation of his world. In a parish it is often the elderly and the housebound who take their place in the front line of God's purposes through prayer and intercession.

An obedient church will be a powerful church. Christians are men and women under authority before they can speak with authority.

Jesus did not say, 'Understand this in remembrance of me'. He said, 'Do it!' So with evangelism. We shall find to our surprise that when we faithfully proclaim his word of good news in obedience to his commands, that lives are changed, things really begin to happen — and all this much to our surprise. The best evangelists are neither the clever nor the eloquent: but simply the faithful and the obedient.

The man who would give orders must, like Peter, first learn to take them.

Stop: Go!

Paul and his companions travelled throughout the region of Phrygia and Galatia, having been kept by the Holy Spirit from preaching the word in the province of Asia. When they came to the border of Mysia, they tried to enter Bithynia, but the Spirit of Jesus would not allow them to. So they passed by Mysia and went down to Troas. During the night Paul had a vision of a man of Macedonia standing and begging him, 'Come over to Macedonia and help us.'

After Paul had seen the vision, we got ready at once to leave for Macedonia, concluding that God had called us to preach the gospel to them.

From Troas we put out to sea and sailed straight for Samothrace, and the next day on to Neapolis. From there we travelled to Philippi, a Roman colony and the leading city of that district of Macedonia. And we stayed there several days.

Acts 16:6—12

EVENT

Often God says 'no' to our whims and wishes, in order that we may say 'yes' to his will. This passage turned out with hindsight to be a strategic turning point in the mission of God's church and its effects have proved to be of the greatest importance in the over-all direction of apostolic mission and evangelism.

First, however, we need to remember that although Macedonia was in what we now call Europe and the Aegean port of Troas was in Asia, in Paul's day both the western and the eastern coastline in the Aegean were all part of the same Roman empire in the first century. It could have seemed to Paul and his companions all rather a fuss about nothing: surely one place is as good as the next.

In fact, of course, evangelizing Macedonia (Greece as we now call it) proved to be with hindsight a strategic entrance through Philippi into Europe and heralded the evangelization of the continent and culture of Europe. In turn, it was through Europe that the other continents of the world were to be missionized and evangelized.

Man proposes: God disposes. We are not told in what way God flashed a red light both in the province of Asia and in the region of Bithynia; we are simply told that Paul and his companions were 'kept from preaching the word in the province of Asia' and that 'the Spirit of Jesus' would not allow them to evangelize in the region of Bithynia respectively.

Two noes and negatives and then a positive invitation to cross from one continent to the other and to help at that very point where east meets west and has done ever since.

Discerning God's will is no easy matter, yet it is crucial in evangelism and the missionary strategy of the church in every age. We need therefore to make several observations.

First, God's 'noes' and negatives are just as much of an answer to our prayers as is his 'yes'. So also the response 'Yes — but not yet'. That is an important and frequent answer to our over-anxious prayers.

Secondly, discerning God's will does not bypass rational processes, though in the end it will always surpass and transcend the cerebral process. The word used in Greek for 'concluding' (verse 10) indicates a long and carefully argued process of discernment in which all the factors (economic, rational, theological, geographical — the whole spectrum of motivations) all converge and come together in one's mind to form a single affirmation. Mindless enthusiasm needs to be checked by the logical processes of the mind — and an informed mind at that.

Finally, although our faith is personal it is never individualistic. Paul related his personal dream and experience to the whole group who came to a common mind and a corporate decision. Common sense, or *ésprit de corps* is not a bad definition of Christian decision-making. Decision-making in the church is personal but it is not individualistic; it is corporate but it is not collective. 'God told me' is a very individualistic, unscriptural, untraditional and ungodly phrase. 'It seemed good to the Holy Spirit and to us' (Acts 15:28) is much more the pattern of decision-making in the church from the earliest times. 'God spake once, and twice have I also heard the same' in the words of the psalmist can be translated — 'God said one thing but I heard two!' So look out!

Decision-making in the church, all the way from the parish level to the level of the national synod, must not simply imitate the processes of political decision-making in which there are winners and losers and majorities and minorities. Many parishes nowadays are organizing parish policy on the basis of unanimous decisions, refusing to take votes and governed by majorities. Many parochial church councils and vestries are willing to wait until a decision can be unanimous before proceeding with a strategic policy. It compels all those taking part to think harder, to pray more earnestly and to be more, not less responsible about their attitude and outlook.

It could be that in our day we shall see the very reversal of Paul's vision. The west has had its chance to declare for Christ. What about the east, the middle east and the orient? Is God beckoning us to look now in that direction, not only for the help we could give but for the help we now need to receive, not least from the persecuted churches of eastern Europe and the developing countries of the south and the east?

Escape or Freedom

FRIDAY   **WEEK 3**

About midnight Paul and Silas were praying and singing hymns to God, and the other prisoners were listening to them. Suddenly there was such a violent earthquake that the foundations of the prison were shaken. At once all the prison doors flew open, and everybody's chains came loose. The jailer woke up, and when he saw the prison doors open, he drew his sword and was about to kill himself because he thought the prisoners had escaped. But Paul shouted, 'Don't harm yourself! We are all here!'

The jailer called for lights, rushed in and fell trembling before Paul and Silas. He then brought them out and asked, 'Sirs, what must I do to be saved?'

They replied, 'Believe in the Lord Jesus, and you will be saved — you and your household.' Then they spoke the word of the Lord to him and to all the others in his house. At that hour of the night the jailer took them and washed their wounds; then immediately he and all his family were baptised. The jailer brought them into his house and set a meal before them; he was filled with joy because he had come to believe in God — he and his whole family.

Acts 16:25–34

EVENT

When most people would be full of self-pity (in prison, in the middle of the night, in pain), Paul and Silas were singing God's praises — and after they had both taken a severe flogging, at that!

Then the second contradiction took place — a contradiction so powerful that it brought the jailer to his knees. After the earthquake, the doors of the prison had broken open and the prisoners found that their chains had broken loose. Everyone was set for escape. That meant death for the prison jailer. But no — the very opposite had happened. The prisoners did not break out, but the love of God broke in that night — into the prison and into the life of the jailer and his household. What a reversal.

Such an unexpected reversal evoked the classic request from the jailer: 'What must I do to be saved?' The classic question gets the classic reply, 'Believe in the Lord Jesus.' Paul and Silas ministered the saving words of God to the jailer and there and then (probably with the same water) Paul and Silas baptised the jailer while the jailer washed their wounds. In the words of Chrysostom, there was mutual ministry that night: 'He washed them and was washed: he washed them from their stripes, himself was washed from his sins.' They ministered Jesus to him; he ministered healing to them. The jailer was classic in every way: he was baptised for ministry. So are we all.

The Christian is called to be larger than life. Resurrection life cannot be contained in the niceties of predictable human behaviour. Sin is predictable: grace always multiplies the options.

Religion of course can always be an escape device — a way of running away from the problem and the pain — 'the opium of the masses'. Yet the record of the saints throughout history is not the story of escapism. Far from running away from life and the conflict, it is the contemplatives throughout history who seem to have got to the heart of the matter. It is the contemplatives who change the world — from Teresa of Avila to Mother Teresa of Calcutta. No one could describe them as escapists. They have not broken out, but rather broken in and where most people have found bondage, they have found freedom — even within the prison houses of this world. You can be in bondage in an open field; you can be free within a prison house. So St Paul and Silas exemplified that quality of freedom which is not determined by external circumstances so much as by internal attitudes. A jailer (yes, of all people) could spot the difference. He did not hold the keys to the freedom of men like Paul and Silas. Clearly the keys to their freedom were in Another's hands and the jailer wanted to know that significant Other to whom Paul and Silas had been praying all night and singing hymns.

EXPERIENCE

Paul, a Roman citizen begins his letter to the Romans, not as you might expect with the words, Paul, 'a freed man of the city of Rome', but rather, Paul, 'a slave of Jesus Christ'. Paul had grasped the paradox of his freedom the day that Jesus grasped hold of him on the Damascus road. On that day he had been running away from his problems, escaping into the activity of trying to do God's job for him. That day he turned round, to discover a new freedom — perfect freedom through service: 'whose service is perfect freedom', we say.

So there was no way that Paul would try to escape that night. Rather we are told that Paul and Silas let themselves be brought out of the prison house by the jailer. Nothing made sense that night, until the jailer met Paul's real Keeper — Jesus Christ.

When the world sees Christians living the paradox of true freedom, they will also ask to be introduced to the Keeper of the keys and want to know the key to our freedom. Then we must be ready to name him unashamedly. And we must so know the word of God and the words of life that we are able to minister comfortable words and the words of assurance to anybody, anywhere, at any time of day or night.

That jailer was baptised for ministry: to be nothing less than Jesus for others. That very night the jailer and his household were enrolled into that same service which is discovered in the end to be perfect and true freedom.

Disturbance

Paul replied, 'Brothers, I did not realize that he was the high priest; for it is written: "Do not speak evil about the ruler of your people."'

Then Paul, knowing that some of them were Sadducees and the others Pharisees, called out in the Sanhedrin, 'My brothers, I am a Pharisee, the son of a Pharisee. I stand on trial because of my hope in the resurrection of the dead.' When he said this, a dispute broke out between the Pharisees and the Sadducees, and the assembly was divided. (The Sadducees say that there is no resurrection, and that there are neither angels nor spirits, but the Pharisees acknowledge them all.)

There was a great uproar, and some of the teachers of the law who were Pharisees stood up and argued vigorously. 'We find nothing wrong with this man,' they said. 'What if a spirit or an angel has spoken to him?' The dispute became so violent that the commander was afraid Paul would be torn to pieces by them. He ordered the troops to go down and take him away from them by force and bring him into the barracks.

The following night the Lord stood near Paul and said, 'Take courage! As you have testified about me in Jerusalem, so you must also testify in Rome.'

Acts 23:5—11

EVENT

It is surely true to say that in Luke's record in the book of Acts, wherever Paul was, there you could be sure to find trouble! In this passage, in just three verses, we are told there was 'great uproar . . . vigorous argument . . . violent dispute' and the possibility that Paul would be torn to pieces. Paul was certainly not the sort of person you would commend for a position of pastor in a local church, let alone unanimously elect as bishop of a diocese! People were always very divided about Paul; they always have been.

The words of Jesus come to mind immediately: 'I did not come to bring peace, but a sword' (Matthew 10:34). For we must face the fact that when the word of the gospel is proclaimed it is divisive — it is the 'double-edged sword' of which the writer to the Hebrews speaks. 'It penetrates even to dividing soul and spirit, joints and marrow; it judges the thoughts and attitudes of the heart' (Hebrews 4:12).

So Paul, eyeing his audience, 'divides to rule'. Paul the Pharisee, believing in the surprises of the supernatural (resurrection, spirits, angels) sees that the crowd is almost evenly divided between Pharisees and Sadducees — those who did and those who did not believe in the resurrection. So he charges straight in. Yet we must notice the substance of Paul's gospel. It is, as it had always been — Jesus and the resurrection.

The gospel is not primarily the good life, moralism, sentimental or judgemental. Everything starts and finishes with that word which is both alpha and omega — Jesus and the resurrection. Without that as the basic premise of Christianity, there is no gospel, no church, no good news.

Of course, such a gospel upsets people. It upsets their intellectual prejudices, their twentieth-century mind-set and their educational upbringing, and above all it upsets 'religious' people who see the church primarily as the moral police force of society. Surely, they will say, we can trim the gospel of some of its more extreme supernatural claims and level with all men of good will to promote a decent, moral way of life.

EXPLANATION

Yet such decaffeinated Christianity, which promises not to keep people awake at night, is in fact impotent to change lives and to change society. Christianity is essentially Jesus and the resurrection — 'a stumbling-block to Jews and foolishness to Gentiles, but to those whom God has called, both Jews and Greeks, Christ the power of God and the wisdom of God' (1 Corinthians 1:23f).

This full-blooded, catholic, scriptural gospel of Jesus Christ is divisive, challenging and disturbing. It cannot be otherwise. Yet only such a gospel, preached fearlessly in the face of opposition, uproar and disturbance, can change the world and save the world.

In his first volume, Luke tells the story of Jesus healing the demoniac from the tiny village community of Gadara. The small population of the area had long since come to terms with the behaviour of the demoniac and now Jesus had upset all that by having the audacity to heal him. A herd of pigs had suddenly rushed headlong over a cliff into the lake and the whole community had been disturbed by this interfering outsider. So Luke tells us: 'Then all the people of the region of the Gerasenes asked Jesus to leave them' (Luke 8:37). How very sensible!

Yet we need to recall that the gospel disturbs the comfortable and at the same time — and often in the same place — it comforts the disturbed.

In these paragraphs we see both sides of this double-edged sword. Here the comfortable are disturbed. And then in the last verse Paul, who must have been deeply disturbed by the events of the day, is wonderfully comforted by the real presence of Jesus, the word of God bringing the comfortable words of direction, assurance and inner security. It is in our communion with Christ that we find that inner peace. 'In the world' we will have tribulation, but we can be of good cheer and take fresh heart, because he has 'overcome the world' (John 16:33). We may not find favour with the crowd — indeed we need to beware when all men 'speak well of us'. We do not need to rely upon opinion polls, for we have found favour with God (as in the case of Mary at the annunciation) because we have been made acceptable in the beloved. That is the good news in a nutshell: it is the news that was brought to Mary by the angel and it is the news which we all need to receive and to know in our inmost hearts. It is the gospel: 'Do not be afraid: God loves you.' At our baptism God looked on us with the same favour as that with which he looked upon Jesus both in his baptism and at his transfiguration. 'Look not on us, but only look on us as found in him' is the charter of all baptised men and women. So there really is nothing to fear. The only trouble is that we would rather find favour with the crowd than with God!

In all this, the scandal of the gospel is unavoidable.

All sorts of things were happening in that little church in Asia
Minor in the early days of Christianity as outlined for us by Luke in
his book of Acts. It had all started in a highly questionable way in
Jerusalem. Things were happening which were deeply disturbing
and which led people from all sorts of backgrounds of all religions
and no religion to ask some very basic questions.

All that was so, because Christianity in those early days was not
so much an idea, but rather an event. Something was happening.
Furthermore it was because something was happening that people
were gossiping. They always gossip when something is happening. Events — good or bad — are a great opportunity. People begin
to ask why and how. It is in response to those questions that we can
gossip the gospel. We are given the opportunity to talk about the
kingdom of God when it is seen in events of the kingdoms of this
world. We can gossip the good news when there is something in
the news worth gossiping about.

All this springs from the central fact of Jesus and the resurrection. All the contradictions of what we like to call miracles are in
keeping with the new way of looking at all things — miracles are the
norm in the kingdom of God. They are only miracles when they
intervene in the kingdoms of this world. The blind see; the deaf
hear; the lame begin to walk — and so it goes on. Mary of course
was on to it at the start with her song — the Magnificat (borrowed of
course from Hannah, who was also on to it centuries earlier). But
on the lips of Peter, in the book of Acts, the claims of the kingdom
are in the present tense: 'He is bringing down the rulers from their
thrones (Herod); he is lifting up the humble (Cornelius, Tabitha).
He is filling the hungry with good things (the beggar at the temple
gate) and the rich he is sending empty away (Ananias).' This is not,
however, a capricious, interfering God who is doing all these

things. Rather this is the power of the kingdom of God breaking into the power structures of this world, so that the most outrageous and incredible contradiction of all is the fact of Jesus and the resurrection.

The church is essentially a kingdom event — demanding that all enquiries look at things in the light of what is already happening in the community of the redeemed.

Furthermore the explanation contains an invitation, not only to come and see for yourself, but also the promise that what has happened in the past and is happening now in the community of faith in the church down the road, could also happen to you and to your 'whole household'. All it requires is the willingness to take a second look, to have second thoughts (repent); to turn around (conversion) and begin to see things backwards from the end to the middle from a new perspective — and all this in the light of Easter morning: the empty tomb and Jesus and the resurrection.

In a sense that is the broad outline of all preaching. Barth used to say that to preach you needed only to take the Bible in one hand and the newspaper in the other — and then make the connection.

We see Peter doing just that in his evangelism, which often occurs after a miracle. We see Philip doing this for the eunuch on the road to Gaza, when the courtier is reading from the book of the prophet Isaiah. We see Paul doing it autobiographically when he explains his conversion on the road to Damascus. Gospel preaching is really gospel explanation of an otherwise inexplicable event.

The essential structure of the explanation is always a story with at least three different dimensions, but in substance the same — the story of Jesus and his love. 'Tell me the old, old story.' That love is made known to us in the shape and profile of death and resurrection — the reversal from death to life. It can start of course with any one of the three dimensions — a story from history (e.g. Isaiah); you could start with a story from a contemporary event (news: the beggar healed in the temple precincts); you could start with your own story (Paul on the Damascus road). All the stories are related to that one story — *the* story of Jesus and the resurrection. Once you see the point of the empty tomb, all the other stories begin to make sense and begin to ring true. Furthermore you know you are standing within inches of the kingdom as the penny drops and the inexplicable at last begin to take shape and make sense. It is not too much to say that at that moment, it is as though scales fall from your eyes (like Paul in Straight Street in Damascus) and you begin to see: not a different world, but the same old world very differently and with a new outlook on the whole of life, because of a new insight.

Question for reflection during the week and for discussion in the group

1.   In what way should the local church be compelling the local community to stop and think?
       In what ways is the local congregation a sign of contradiction or does it just conform to the norm and the expected?
2.   What is my story?
       Do I have one?
       Do I ever tell it or share it with others?
3.   'Christians are hypocrites, pretending to be what they are not.' What truth is there in that statement?

Relating the Facts of the Case

'Men of Israel, listen to this: Jesus of Nazareth was a man accredited by God to you by miracles, wonders and signs, which God did among you through him, as you yourselves know. This man was handed over to you by God's set purpose and foreknowledge; and you, with the help of wicked men, put him to death by nailing him to the cross. But God raised him from the dead, freeing him from the agony of death, because it was impossible for death to keep its hold on him.

'. . . God has raised this Jesus to life, and we are all witnesses of the fact. Exalted to the right hand of God, he has received from the Father the promised Holy Spirit and has poured out what you now see and hear.'

'. . . Therefore let all Israel be assured of this: God has made this Jesus, whom you crucified, both Lord and Christ.'

Acts 2:22—24, 32—33, 36

EVENT

The work of the church in every generation and in all nations is to present Jesus: to represent Jesus and re-present him through the three-fold witness of the word, the sacraments and life in the Spirit. 'Sirs, we would see Jesus,' is the request of the Greeks to the apostles. The Gentile world and those outside the church have continued to repeat that question either implicitly or explicitly ever since. (John 12:21 — 'Sirs, it is Jesus we want to see!') The church must never forget that: not some programme, ideology or set of rules, nor any thing of however great value — no *thing* but some *body* — Jesus.

So the first Christian sermon, after the opening greetings, begins with the word 'Jesus'. Jesus is the first word on the lips of the church and the last 'this Jesus . . .'

Which Jesus? For there were many Jesuses in Jerusalem in the days of Jesus of Nazareth: Jesus Bar Abbas, for example. And there are many Jesuses being presented today, so the problem is still the same: the Jesus that the church proclaims must be the Jesus of history — the one who worked 'miracles, wonders and signs' as happened in history. He is the same Jesus as the one who was crucified under Pontius Pilate, died and was buried; the same Jesus as was raised and exalted as both Lord and Christ.

There was no escape from just telling the 'old, old story of Jesus and his love'.

All this, though taking place in time and in space, has lasting significance and implications beyond time and space, and for eternity. The Old Testament, through the prophets and the spiritual yearnings of the Psalms, reached out and pointed forward to such a figure as would give hope and meaning to the meaningless sufferings of the Old Testament; victory for the many defeats and disasters of the old Israel.

All this account is true, objectively. But then the messenger, the preacher and the witness must go further. He or she has to witness to the fact that they found it to be true in giving meaning to their own lives and deepening their experiences. The story of history becomes their story. It rings true: it is not just history or the Jesus story (though it is both of these things). It is *my* story: it resonates with the most profound experience within *my* life.

Making that connection is essentially the work of the Holy Spirit. The Holy Spirit makes Jesus present and makes the connection deep within the hearts of the hearers between his story and their story. When such preaching is empowered and anointed by the Spirit of God it always 'cuts to the heart' (2:37) and leads to repentance: a new outlook because of a new insight.

Our part in all of this is to witness — to tell our story from our point of view and then to leave the Holy Spirit to make the connection. He made the connections on the feast of Pentecost and he has been doing just that ever since.

EXPERIENCE

The church in our day must recover a new love for the very name of Jesus. His name should be on our lips because he has first found a place in our hearts. Our sermons, our witnessing and our lives need to be ever more Christo-centric.

Secondly, we must invoke the Holy Spirit at all times to do his work of representing Jesus and making him present and contemporary in our world (John 14:26). In most of the apostolic sermons as recorded in Acts, Luke nearly always tells us that the preacher was full of the Holy Spirit. (He does not need to do this on the day of Pentecost having already told us only a few verses earlier of the coming of the Spirit to the apostles gathered together in that upper room. On that one occasion we can take it for granted, but we should not, and Luke certainly does not on nearly every other occasion when there is the record of witnessing, proclamation, preaching or testimony — Acts 4:31; 7:55; 10:44; 13:9; 13:52.)

Thirdly we must present the gospel as personal. While recording the objectivity of the story of history and the story of Jesus, it must be endorsed by our personal witness — 'and we are all witnesses of the fact'. Every confirmation sermon or evangelistic address should include a personal witness in the course of the sermon either by the preacher or by someone else.

Finally the conclusion of the sermon should be sufficiently pointed that it demands a response of some kind from the hearers. Like lightning, all good preaching finds the earth and cuts to the heart not in a wounding or bullying way but certainly in a challenging and necessarily disturbing way.

Such is the content and calibre then of apostolic preaching in the book of Acts. How does our witness and preaching measure up to that? It certainly had an effect and was effective preaching. Does ours? If not, why not?

Christianity or Churchianity?

While the beggar held on to Peter and John, all the people were astonished and came running to them in the place called Solomon's Colonnade. When Peter saw this, he said to them: 'Men of Israel, why does this surprise you? Why do you stare at us as if by our own power or godliness we had made this man walk? The God of Abraham, Isaac and Jacob, the God of our fathers, has glorified his servant Jesus. You handed him over to be killed, and you disowned him before Pilate, though he had decided to let him go. You disowned the Holy and Righteous One and asked that a murderer be released to you. You killed the author of life, but God raised him from the dead. We are witnesses of this. By faith in the name of Jesus, this man whom you see and know was made strong. It is Jesus' name and the faith that comes through him that has given this complete healing to him, as you can all see.'

Acts 3:11—16

EVENT

The scene is all too clear. At centre of stage are Peter and John. The beggar, although he is healed, free and perfectly able to walk is still holding to Peter and John. He cannot take his eyes off them. On the other side stands the curious, astonished crowd, running through the cloister-like 'portico' (REB) of Solomon's Colonnade, which ran along the eastern side of the outer court of the temple — incidentally, the very area of the temple precincts in which Jesus had walked and talked. It was in that very spot that a similar crowd had gathered only months before to ask Jesus about his miracles. On that occasion, Jesus had directed their attention away from himself to his Father in whose name he spoke (John 10:22—30).

Peter and John are faced with a similar problem. The crowd and the beggar are both alike 'staring' at Peter and John as if by their 'own power or godliness' they had made the man walk (verse 12). That explanation will not do. Peter has the text and the setting for an evangelistic sermon. Something has happened and it needs now to be explained. So Peter is going to hold up Jesus as the Christ, the Servant, the Holy One and source of all life — the Prophet and the Stone — and all the great biblical titles, which prove that Jesus is the root cause of this whole event. It is to Jesus — the Jesus whom the crowd has rejected — it is to this Jesus that all power must be ascribed. Peter and John are merely witnesses and as such they must get away from the centre of the stage. The attention of both the beggar and the crowd must be redirected to Jesus, the unseen, leading character in this whole dramatic event. And then those who have rejected Jesus and chosen the wrong Jesus (Barabbas) would have another chance to declare for the right Jesus — Jesus the Christ — as the challenge is put to them. They can choose God's own choice.

EXPLANATION

When John the Baptist was in prison we are told that he lost his nerve and sent the disciples to enquire whether or not Jesus was the Christ. The reply of Jesus is most interesting. He did not send back a list of his credentials or an essay on christology. Instead, he told the enquirers to go back to John and to tell him what they had seen and heard and what was happening around Jesus. The blind were seeing, the lame were walking and all the other contradictory features of the coming of the kingdom as described by Isaiah (chapter 61) were happening under their very noses.

The church, in other words, is intended to be the arena in which the signs of the kingdom are evident. Such a church makes the task of the preacher much easier: he has simply to explain what is happening and attribute it to Jesus and the resurrection. Furthermore witnesses can say to their friends, 'come and see' (John 1:39, 46), for we cannot but speak of the things 'we have seen and heard' (Acts 4:20). But then when people come to see, they must be able to see right through the church! They must be able to see Jesus and be challenged to choose him whom they previously rejected as the author of life — real life, resurrection life, abundant life, the sort of life which gives sight to the blind and enables lame people to walk.

EXPERIENCE

A truly apostolic church will always point to Jesus and the resurrection and ascribe to him the glory and the praise for all his wonderous works. It will never allow faith in Jesus to degenerate into faith in his church: it will never substitute churchianity for Christianity! It will never substitute counselling for gospelling and so will not permit pastoral dependency to take over where truth, healing and freedom should reign supreme. The apostolic church will stubbornly and consistently minister Jesus to people, both personally and corporately through word, sacrament and life in the Spirit. An apostolic church will refuse to use earthly power in the shape of money ('silver or gold'); the manipulation of the crowd or the power of the spectacular. It will point only to Jesus, crucified, raised and glorified. An apostolic church will fulfil the only criterion to be truly apostolic, namely by witnessing to Jesus and his resurrection. Such a church will have a record of saving events, a story to tell, a song to sing and a life to live. In some sense such a church will be strangely irresistible.

Professionals and Unprofessionals

TUESDAY   **WEEK 4**

They had Peter and John brought before them and began to question them: 'By what power or what name did you do this?'

Then Peter, filled with the Holy Spirit, said to them: 'Rulers and elders of the people! If we are being called to account today for an act of kindness shown to a cripple and are asked how he was healed, then know this, you and all the people of Israel: It is by the name of Jesus Christ of Nazareth, whom you crucified but whom God raised from the dead, that this man stands before you healed. He is

'"the stone you builders rejected
which has become the capstone."

Salvation is found in no one else, for there is no other name under heaven given to men by which we must be saved.'

When they saw the courage of Peter and John and realized that they were unschooled, ordinary men, they were astonished and they took note that these men had been with Jesus.

Acts 4:7—13

EVENT

All the top brass were there!The Sanhedrin was the supreme court of the Jews. It had seventy-one members and was presided over by the high priest who was ex-officio a member of the priestly court. Luke spells it out. The 'rulers' were there and 'the elders' and the 'teachers of the law'. But, Luke goes on, Annas the high priest was there. He was no longer officially the high priest, as he had been deposed by the Romans in AD 15, but he was still the power behind the throne. Caiaphas was there, son-in-law to Annas. But there were still some more — they came out of the woodwork that day! John and Alexander — all members of the high priestly family, the extended mafia of the priestly clan of Sadducees and Pharisees — they were there. It was a formidable array that greeted Peter and John and the healed man — that well-known sight in the temple precincts for some forty years.

The trouble was that the man was now walking. There was no way to refute that kind of evidence or rig the truth as that self-same court had done only months before, in the case of Jesus. It had all taken place, right there in the temple precincts and five thousand men (let alone women and children) had declared themselves as believers in the past twenty-four hours.

Peter and John's mind must have flashed back to a similar scene only months earlier when Jesus was on trial, then led from this group to Pilate and to crucifixion. On that occasion Peter and John had been outsiders, in the courtyard as observers, and Peter had denied Christ. This time they were right at the centre of the stage standing where Jesus had stood. This time however, Peter would not deny Christ, but confess him.

We must further recall that John would be a young boy of nineteen or so at the most. Both Peter and John were fishermen from Galilee, 'unschooled', 'ordinary men' who spoke with a northern accent so despised by the southerners from the metropolis of Jerusalem. Notice, Luke tells us that while Peter was eloquent and articulate in his defence with the lame man 'standing there', right next to him, the learned and professional felt 'there was nothing they could say'. Peter's tongue was remarkably loose that day: they were tongue-tied. When Jesus had stood there — it seemed like yesterday — he was silent and Caiaphas and Annas and all the rest of the tribe did all the talking. Now the tables are turned; the professionals are silent. Peter and John (and the healed man by his very presence) — all unprofessionals — are eloquent in their witness to Jesus, making out a perfectly cogent case for the healing and the resurrection.

EXPERIENCE

Clearly the Sanhedrin and the professionals had to wrestle with all this. So do we. First, we need to notice that Luke specifically tells us that Peter was 'filled with the Holy Spirit'. Secondly, this scene took place after Peter and John had witnessed resurrection. Thirdly, as the Sanhedrin observed, these men had spent time with Jesus and clearly something 'rubbed off'. Finally, this was clearly an example of what Jesus himself had promised: 'They will deliver you to synagogues and prisons, and you will be brought before kings and governors, and all on account of my name,' Luke significantly records in his first volume. 'This will result in your being witnesses to them. But make up your mind not to worry beforehand how you will defend yourselves. For I will give you words and wisdom that none of your adversaries will be able to resist or contradict' (Luke 21:12ff). Yes, there it was happening before their very eyes.

For witnessing is not just for the educated, professionals with a theological training — though the church needs them also. But it is for all Christians, professional and unprofessional, providing they have the following qualifications. We must experience Pentecost 'daily' and 'increase in his Holy Spirit more and more'. We must also have witnessed resurrection at work in our own lives — firsthand evidence. We must rely upon the Holy Spirit to loosen our tongues rather than to prepare set speeches or prototypes of witness — simply tell our own story. And finally we must spend time with Jesus — in his school — and then something of him will rub off on us also. That sort of church — clergy and laity, professional and unprofessional, the silent (the cured beggar) and the eloquent — all will constitute an evangelizing church and nothing will be able to withstand that sort of evidence.

The Test of Time

When they heard this, they were furious and wanted to put them to death. But a Pharisee named Gamaliel, a teacher of the law, who was honoured by all the people, stood up in the Sanhedrin and ordered that the men be put outside for a little while. Then he addressed them: 'Men of Israel, consider carefully what you intend to do to these men. Some time ago Theudas appeared, claiming to be somebody, and about four hundred men rallied to him. He was killed, all his followers were dispersed, and it all came to nothing. After him, Judas the Galilean appeared in the days of the census and led a band of people in revolt. He too was killed, and all his followers were scattered. Therefore, in the present case I advise you: Leave these men alone! Let them go! For if their purpose or activity is of human origin, it will fail. But if it is from God, you will not be able to stop these men; you will only find yourselves fighting against God.'

Acts 5:33—39

Earlier warnings and a flogging by the Sanhedrin had failed to silence the apostles in Jerusalem and the number of believers was growing daily. Clearly things were getting out of hand. More and more people were added to their number (5:14) and the apostles were filling Jerusalem with their teaching (verse 28) — and always the same, namely about that Jesus and his resurrection. Something had to be done — and soon. The Sanhedrin had to come to a decision and to have an official line about this new and — potentially — revolutionary movement.

At that moment Gamaliel, a highly respected member of the Sanhedrin stood up to speak. He was, Luke tells us, 'honoured by all the people,' 'a Pharisee' and 'a teacher of the law,' very much the elder statesman. As a Pharisee he would be less intolerant than members of the majority party, the Sadducees, with this new group and their teaching about the resurrection. Furthermore, he was the grandson and disciple of the famous liberal Rabbi Hillel and we know from later in Luke's record that Saul of Tarsus had, in his early life been one of his pupils (22:3).

Gamaliel brought an air of wisdom and sanity to their deliberations. His argument was a purely pragmatic one. Palestine at that time was overrun with religious and political movements and with charismatic leaders who had quite a following — Theudas and Judas to name just two recent ones. Josephus, the Jewish historian, tells us specifically that around this time and after the death of Herod, 'There were ten thousand other disorders in Judea, which were like tumults' (*Antiquities* 17.10.4). If this latest rising of the apostles was simply another of these and if it was purely 'of human origin', then it would soon die out, as all the others had. If of course, it was 'from God', then you could not stop it and indeed you would find yourself actively persecuting the early Christian church and 'fighting against God'. In other words, let us see what the test of time will do.

EXPLANATION

It is true of course that truth stands the test of time, but over the short run evil can triumph and fads, fashions and vogues tend to have their little day. Gamaliel was not saying that whatever will be will be — for that would be determinism. As a good Pharisee, believing in the God of history, Gamaliel could never have totally subscribed to such a *laissez-faire* point of view. He is rather taking the long look and the fuller perspective which a view of history can give. The God of history has the last word and generally time will tell a great deal both about a person, a movement or a discovery. A mere flash in the pan need not really disturb the Sanhedrin at all.

EXPERIENCE

So then what about the privileged perspective of two thousand years of Christianity which we enjoy today? Again and again over the centuries, tyrants have attempted to kill the church and again and again thoughout history prophets of doom have prophesied the immediate and ultimate demise of the church. At the close of the twentieth century and taking an overall view, Christianity is the most rapidly growing religion in the world today. Jesus Christ is amazingly alive for someone whom many would want to write off as a wise, eccentric rabbi who was unjustly put to death two thousand years ago. Nobody has written a musical on Theudas or Judas! It takes intricate scholarship to dig their names out of the dust of libraries and museums. After seventy-three years of Communist oppression, the church is being raised up again in Soviet Russia, churches are opening and seminaries and monasteries are full to overflowing. If Jesus Christ is dead, why on earth will he not lie down?

The best proof of the resurrection of Jesus two thousand years ago, is a living church today. Try explaining it any other way. Gamaliel proved to be more right than perhaps he ever realized — for the onus of explanation for a living, expanding world-wide church today is now upon the shoulders of *unbelievers,* atheists and agnostics. It is up to them to try to explain it in sound logical terms and to answer Gamaliel's challenge.

It is hard to over-estimate the witness of a lively, growing church community in a village, town or city: its very existence tells the story. But only, of course, if the church community is really alive and kicking.

The Challenge of Painful Truth

'You stiff-necked people, with uncircumcised hearts and ears! You are just like your fathers: You always resist the Holy Spirit! Was there ever a prophet your fathers did not persecute! They even killed those who predicted the coming of the Righteous One. And now you have betrayed and murdered him — you have received the law that was put into effect through angels but have not obeyed it.'

Acts 7:51—53

EVENT

They could not see the wood for the trees. Stephen, in his defence, plays back to the Jewish leaders their own history, seen from the point of view of its fulfilment in Jesus Christ. Jesus, on the road to Emmaus, undertook a very similar exercise with Cleopas and his friend — 'beginning with Moses and all the prophets,' explaining 'to them what was said in all the scriptures concerning himself' (Luke 24:27). When you re-read the scriptures from the vantage point of Jesus Christ and with the advantage of hindsight, surely it is staring you in the face. Jesus of Nazareth was the One to whom all the scriptures, the prophets, Abraham, Moses, Joseph and David had pointed. It was all only too self-evident.

Equally evident, however, was the blindness, disobedience and resistance of the Jewish people to the teaching of the prophets. Throughout their privileged history they had been consistently stiff-necked, blind and unteachable. Yet this was the tragedy, namely that God's chosen people who had been groomed and schooled for hundreds of years for this very moment in history should, when the moment came and the promised one had arrived, not only have failed to recognize him but actually have sought to destroy him. It has to be one of the great tragedies of the world.

EXPLANATION

This radical re-writing of their history certainly got the Jewish leaders on the raw. Truth often hurts. 'Human kind cannot bear very much reality' (T.S. Eliot). Jesus had challenged the Jewish leaders with a similar re-casting of their history in the parable of the vineyard. In Luke's gospel it is told at some length and comes as the climax to Jesus' confrontation with the 'teachers of the law and chief priests', who were now bent on the destruction of Jesus, 'because they knew he had spoken this parable against them' (Luke 20:19). Stephen refused to pull any punches. His re-working of the history of revelation showed up the Jewish nation in a very bad light. He was not condemning them: on the contrary, they were to condemn him. But he was challenging them in such a way that they could not simply shrug their shoulders and walk away indifferently. There were only two options for Stephen's audience on that day. Either they would have to 'repent', take a second look at their record, have second thoughts and review the whole situation; or they would have to destroy Stephen. In the end, for all of us, there are only two responses to good gospel preaching: *metanoia* or paranoia. Either you will hear the preacher as speaking for you, or you will suppose he is speaking against you. Either you will be led to give your life to Jesus, or you will go on and seek to take his. Only in that sense is it all give and take.

Teilhard de Chardin says that in the end we have only two choices: adoration or annihilation. Gospel preaching is not intended to whip up guilt: Stephen did not condemn his persecutors. On the contrary, he died praying for them and pleading for their forgiveness. However, when Jesus, the truth, is held up to people, they have to respond and it is always the same alternative: hosanna or crucify. There really is not much middle ground in 'give or take'.

Saul had been listening in on the edge of the crowd. His first response at the time of the death of Stephen was a kind of half-hearted 'crucify'. He stood as near as anyone could on the middle ground of consent, holding the clothes — yet by saying nothing he was in fact saying no. All that is required for evil to triumph is for good men to say nothing. Yet by God's grace Paul had second thoughts (he repented) and he ended up by shouting with every fibre of his being, 'Hosanna!'

All apostolic preaching and presentation of the gospel are intended to come to the point of choice. We preach for repentance. That's the point of preaching, yet so often, like those Jews of old, religious people are in danger of missing the point of it all!

Reading the Signposts

Then Philip ran up to the chariot and heard the man reading Isaiah the prophet. 'Do you understand what you are reading?' Philip asked.

'How can I,' he said, 'unless someone explains it to me?' So he invited Philip to come up and sit with him.

The eunuch was reading this passage of Scripture: 'He was led like a sheep to the slaughter . . .'

The eunuch asked Philip, 'Tell me, please, who is the prophet talking about, himself or someone else?' Then Philip began with that very passage of Scripture and told him the good news about Jesus.

As they travelled along the road, they came to some water and the eunuch said, 'Look, here is water. Why shouldn't I be baptised?' And he gave orders to stop the chariot. Then both Philip and the eunuch went down into the water and Philip baptised him.

Acts 8:30—32, 34—38

EVENT

'Blessed Lord, you have caused all holy scriptures to be written for our learning' we pray in the special scriptural collect. Notice we refer to 'all holy scriptures' — Old and New Testament alike. The scriptures, like the sacraments, are a gift from God to his church to help us to learn the mind of Christ.

Philip, like the good preacher or Bible teacher, is driven by the Holy Spirit. He has eyes to see the signposts and to make the connection between the 'there-and-then' passage of scripture and the 'here-and-now' of Christian discipleship. 'Is there a word of the Lord for us, today?' asks Zedekiah of the prophet Jeremiah. There is

— there always is — but sometimes we need the Spirit-driven teacher to bring us to where that word is and so make it alive for us at all times and in all places.

'Tell me, please,' says the eunuch, 'who is the prophet talking about, himself or someone else?' The answer is at least two-dimensional and will need to become three-dimensional if the word of scripture is to come alive for that eunuch on that day on that road between Jerusalem and Gaza.

The suffering servant, the innocent, redemptively suffering victim, had its place in the history of Isaiah's day, either in his own or another's biography. Jesus, we know from the gospels, took that same passage and applied it to his own identity, seeing something of his own vocation and destiny in the light of that passage from Isaiah written hundreds of years earlier. So Philip, steeped in the tradition of the Jews makes the connection for the eunuch, beginning 'with that very passage of Scripture and told him the good news about Jesus' (verse 35).

EXPLANATION

What would be the core of that 'good news about Jesus'? Surely it would be easy to start with the passage concerning the suffering servant, 'once upon a time' and move from there to the 'once for all' story of the death and resurrection of Jesus, speaking of 'his humiliation' which was indeed 'deprived of justice'? However, undoubtedly Philip did not stop there, because Isaiah does not have the last word on this as on anything else. For the last word is not humiliation but exaltation: this same Jesus, who was unjustly abused and killed, God has raised and highly exalted. Furthermore, it is through faith in his name that humiliation, disaster and injustice do not constitute the last words for us. God wishes to bring us together with Jesus and that eunuch through the valley of humiliation and to raise us up in his Son — providing we believe and trust in Christ as our Lord and saviour and are baptised into the likeness of his death and resurrection. Philip, with the help of the Holy Spirit, made the connection between three stories: history, the Jesus story and the story of that eunuch.

So in a sense, with the help of the Holy Spirit to make the connection, Isaiah is talking (unwittingly) about a third person — that eunuch. In some sense that anonymous figure from the centuries BC, Jesus of Nazareth and the eunuch from Ethiopia of the first century AD share together a similar identity. That passage from Isaiah rang bells for that eunuch on that day on that road. As a courtier and necessarily therefore as eunuch, in the service of a potentate, he had known his fair share of humiliation and injustice, so in language which is deliberatley the language of death and resurrection Luke tells us of the eunuch's baptism.

We need not only the gift of the scriptures to read, mark, learn and inwardly digest; we also need the gift of good Bible teachers, who are text-driven and Spirit-driven to help serious inquirers to make the connection. That is a precious and important ministry. Furthermore, we need to read the scriptures in that three-dimensional way which makes the connections of identity anywhere in time and space, summoning men and women from every race, colour and age to become men and women of the resurrection — men and women who have the mind and outlook of Christ and who share in the identity of Christ: the mystery of his suffering, death and resurrection.

If the eunuch began his journey that day from Jerusalem to Gaza with something of an identity crisis, we can be certain that when he came up out of the waters of baptism and got back into his chariot, he knew not only who he was but also whose he was. The scriptures are a map for disciples and for men and women who want to travel. We also need the guidance of the Holy Spirit that comes to us in the form of Bible teachers, guides, men and women of scriptural experience who can read and interpret the signposts for us.

Christianity and Other Religions

Paul then stood up in the meeting of the Areopagus and said: 'Men of Athens! I see that in every way you are very religious. For as I walked around and looked carefully at your objects of worship, I even found an altar with this inscription: TO AN UNKNOWN GOD. Now what you worship as something unknown I am going to proclaim to you.

'The God who made the world and everything in it is the Lord of heaven and earth and does not live in temples built by hands. And he is not served by human hands, as if he needed anything, because he himself gives all men life and breath and everything else. From one man he made every nation of men, that they should inhabit the whole earth; and he determined the times set for them and the exact places where they should live. God did this so that men would seek him and perhaps reach out for him and find him, though he is not far from each one of us. "For in him we live and move and have our being." As some of your own poets have said, "We are his offspring."

'Therefore since we are God's offspring, we should not think that the divine being is like gold or silver or stone — an image made by man's design and skill. In the past God overlooked such ignorance, but now he commands all people everywhere to repent. For he has set a day when we will judge the world with justice by the man he has appointed. He has given proof of this to all men by raising him from the dead.'

Acts 17:22—31

For a while Paul was on his own in Athens — the intellectual metropolis of the ancient world. He walked around the city, through the market place and public square (the Agora); looking up to the Acropolis where the great statue and temple of Athena (the Parthenon) dominated the sky-line across to the north-west of the Acropolis to the Areopagus or Mars Hill, where the venerable judicial court of ancient Athens and Greece met. He 'did' Athens while he was waiting for Silas and Timothy to join him as soon as possible (verses 15f).

We read 'he was greatly distressed to see that the city was full of idols'. The Greek word used is found nowhere else in the New Testament, not indeed anywhere else in the whole of Greek literature and is perhaps best translated as 'smothered with idols,' 'swamped in idols' or as one translator puts it, 'a veritable forest of idols'. Indeed we know from the writings of a second-century Greek tourist Pausanias that from the earliest times there were a large number of temples and shrines near the harbour in ancient Greece, together with 'altars and to gods named unknown'. It was presumably one such altar which Paul came across when he set out on his tour of Athens.

He began in the synagogue with the Jews and God-fearing Greeks and went also each day to the market-place where he gossiped the gospel with the Epicurean and Stoic philosophers. From there he was taken to Mars Hill where he was given the opportunity to address a formal meeting of the Areopagus. In a word, he evangelized the city of Athens, all the way from the 'church-goers' (the synagogue) to the market-place and from the market-place to the university and the corridors of intellectual and political power.

Paul started his evangelism where people were. There is no other place to start. He was greatly put out by the superstition, the religiosity and multiplicity of deities. He did not, however, sweep all that away and accuse them of going over the top in their undirected religious enthusiasm. Indeed he did not accuse them of going too far at all but rather of not going far enough. Their gods were not only too many but they were also too small, by half!

Beginning with a text from a shrine — 'to an unknown god' — he moved from what they knew to what they did not know; from where they were to where they should be. He met them on their own terms and on their ground — literally — whether it was in the synagogue, the market-place or the Areopagus. His evangelism was targeted and so must ours be if we are to reach not only church-goers but others.

Yet what about Christianity and the unknown god of Hinduism and the religions of the world? For them and for all religions, Paul has a word: 'What you worship as some*thing* unknown,' I will now declare to you as some*one* who has made himself known.

EXPERIENCE

'All roads lead to God': that is sentimental nonsense; it is as senti-mental and dangerous as to suppose that enthusiasm and sincerity would be all that would be needed to climb Mount Everest. Nevertheless, all serious seekers lead to the Word (or *logos* in John's language). That is the latent, hidden, anonymous foundation of the whole universe. There are all kinds of 'Old Testaments' which are (or can be) 'tutors' to bring us to Christ — the *logos*. But there is only one Christ who can bring us to the Father. Furthermore, that jour-ney is not *straightforward*. When the witness of what I choose to call the many old testaments of religion brings people to Christ (or rather when Christ comes out to meet them), they need to be con-verted before they can go on in Christ and be brought into union with the Father. Fundamentally, that journey is not simply a ques-tion of more and more knowledge *about* God. Rather the journey of faith (all faiths) is intended to culminate in Christ (and only *in him*) in communion and in love within the blessed Trinity. Knowledge about God needs to be superseded by communion with God and that is only possible in Christ.

Real evangelism will not be afraid of the multiplicity of religious alternatives, idolatries and the pantheon of gods which we find in all great cities to this day. Rather, we need, like St Paul, to take the trouble to linger and 'loiter with intent' in the synagogues and with the God-fearers; to go into the shopping malls, pubs and clubs, the winebars and all the public places where people talk — and to share the agendas of their hearts and minds. But we need to go further and to be ready to engage in serious, thoughtful dialogue with serious minded and thoughtful scholars, university faculties and the leaders of our society. In all these engagements we must be neither sentimental nor judgemental. Our response needs to be 'Yes, but . . .' as we seek to uncover the mystery of God's revelation, hidden within every atom and molecule of the known world. Evangelism does not render education and dialogue obsolete: on the contrary, it is always willing like Christ on the Emmaus road 'to go further'. The church, of course, has very little to say to the flippant, the neophiliacs and those who love to talk for talking's sake (verse 21), but there will always be some serious seekers in every ghetto of the city and like Paul we must care enough to go and seek them out. We need like Paul the motivation of nothing less than passion for souls, if people are to be moved from the swapping of opinions to convictions and commitment.

'The Lord added to their number' is the recurring coda to many of those apostolic acts as recorded by Luke in his book of Acts. By word and by deed, through word and through sacrament and life in the Spirit, the apostles continued a threefold witness to Jesus and the resurrection all around Asia Minor and beyond; and again and again we are told that the Lord went before them and followed after them, both preparing and consolidating. In the memorable words of Charles Williams, Jesus went before them and after them 'scattering promises of power' here, there and everywhere. It was indeed a springtime for loving and believing with flowers of resurrection life springing up in the most unlikely deserts and unpromising terrain.

But we must notice that the apostles did not go out primarily to make members of the church — they did not go scalp-hunting! As we shall see in the last week of our Bible studies, the church was the inevitable expression of the gospel: the disciples did not see church membership as the goal, but rather as an inevitable by-product — namely what happens when people hear and *receive* the word of God.

Christianity was not so much a matter of going to church but rather a whole new way of seeing the whole of life — a life lived as a member of the body of Christ, formed and fashioned by the work of the Holy Spirit, which indwells God's people and so draws them together in a single communion of love and faith.

Evangelization is essentially presenting, by word and deed, Jesus and his resurrection. Often in the book of Acts we do not know if anybody responded to the gospel at all. We are told that Philip evangelized the towns of Samaria but we are not told what the response was. God is Lord of the harvest. Our only care is to take heed 'to right sowing'. An over-concern with numbers leads to that manipulative evangelization which is soon shot through with pride and self-aggrandisement.

We must learn to rest in the Lord and to trust in him. It is his church. Numbers are not our prime concern — God is the chief evangelist. It is his church and we have his promise that that church will prevail against all odds.

So we must not talk in terms of success and failure in evangelism. Such words do not belong to the vocabulary of the kingdom. However, we can and we should talk of fruitful evangelism, because a word anointed with the Spirit of God goes forth from God's mouth and it does 'not return' empty (Isaiah 55).

Eloquence, a good mind and powerful speech all have their place in evangelism. Yet Paul is insistent: 'My message and my preaching were not with wise and persuasive words, but with a demonstration of the Spirit's power, so that your faith might not rest on men's wisdom, but on God's power' (1 Corinthians 2:4f). We do not need to be clever to commend Christ to others, nor do preachers need to be eloquent with words. But disciples, witnesses, preachers and evangelists alike do need to be anointed with the power of the Holy Spirit — that is the true power of persuasion.

Furthermore there is a special timing in all of God's designs. The seed sown may not bring forth a harvest in the lifetime of the sower. One sows and another reaps, but 'neither he who plants, nor he who waters is anything, but only God who makes things grow' (1 Corinthians 3:7) — and always in his good time: God's time, high time!

Just because we believe the Lord is calling his church to a special time of evangelization (the so-called Decade of Evangelism), it does not follow that there will necessarily be an increase in church membership. It is to be a decade when we give special attention to sowing the word. The harvest from that sowing may not be reaped in the last decade of this century. We may not live to see the harvest at all.

So we shall not speak of success or failure at the beginning, during or at the conclusion of the decade; but only seek to speak ever more truly of the gospel and the kingdom in words which we pray will indeed be anointed with power — a power to change people's lives. When, wherever and to what extent that happens will, hopefully, show up in church attendance and statistics, but we must not let our eyes or our gaze be trapped on those figures or with those concerns. Our concern is to be where the Lord would have us as 'God's fellow workers'; to be in the right place at the right time saying the right things. In such a missionary church, whether there are few or many need not be our concern.

Questions for reflection during the week and for discussion in the group

1. Is the local congregation the sort of church to which the Lord could add new Christians? Do we really want the local church to grow?
2. Barnabas means 'the son of encouragement'. Do we encourage each other and especially the clergy, in times of disappointment and dwindling numbers?
3. The ministry of intercession is the work of God's fellow workers, preparing the field for the seed of the word. Am I praying for the conversion of my god-children, my friends or loved ones who as yet do not know the Lord?
4. Am I willing to make a fool of myself to follow a hunch by speaking of faith or doing some ministry to someone because I feel the Lord is seeking out a particular person? Am I willing to be an agent for God in *his* evangelization?

Facts and Faith

The priests and the captain of the temple guard and the Sadducees came up to Peter and John while they were speaking to the people. They were greatly disturbed because the apostles were teaching the people and proclaiming in Jesus the resurrection of the dead. They seized Peter and John, and because it was evening, they put them in jail until the next day. But many who heard the message believed, and the number . . . grew to about five thousand.

Acts 4:1—4

EVENT

The church grew because it was rooted and grounded in right belief — belief in Jesus and the resurrection. Naturally the Sadducees were 'greatly disturbed' by this new teaching, because their belief did not permit any possibility of resurrection. There was no room left in their view of the universe for surprises. (That's the reason the Sadducees were so sad, you see!)

But then Peter and John in their preaching did not set out to proclaim an all-inclusive gospel. Their gospel was sharp-edged and radical. Because of what had happened to somebody somewhere, once upon a time (Jesus, the empty tomb, about AD 30), they believed that resurrection could now happen to everybody, everywhere all the time, to the end of time. But notice the basis of their argument.

In a sense the Sadducees were right as far as they went. In their view of the universe they did not have any evidence for resurrection. The universe that they examined showed all the signs of death: everything about the human race from its toenails to its eyebrows was clearly dying from the moment of birth. So little wonder that they had no place for the sentimentality of some kinds of vague doctrine of immortality which haunted the ancient world.

In that sense the Sadducees were realists. The apostles came into that situation with new evidence, however, of a 'new virus' at work in the universe. This new quality of life, unlike bacteria, spreading generally through the human race, needed to be 'hosted' in a cell of personal faith — faith in the new order of things, summed up in the phrase 'Jesus and the resurrection'. So the five thousand new Christians mentioned by Luke were primarily not a matter of church growth. The figure represented rather five thousand people whose minds and hearts had been opened by new evidence on the human case — the evidence of Jesus and the resurrection.

After all, he had died in view of all the people and he had hung there for hour after hour. But in this case there was actual evidence that he had been raised, and furthermore there were witnesses at hand ready to put their lives on the line in their conviction that a new way of seeing things was breaking into history and into the structure of the universe. Such evidence was necessarily deeply disturbing.

EXPLANATION

In some ways the radical Sadducees were nearer the kingdom in their approach than the sentimentality of our contemporary, secular world. They cared about the truth and they saw to it that in the end the whole stood or fell not on uninformed opinions but on convictions tempered by new evidence. Their foolishness lay not in their convictions but in their wish to suppress the new evidence.

Notice that the resurrection of the dead that the disciples were proclaiming was not based upon feelings about death, the dying or the dead. It was based upon a new order of things made possible only *in Jesus*. 'This is eternal life,' says Jesus, to know God and him whom he has sent (John 17:3). Eternal life is a quality of life which is essentially friendship with God made possible only to those who *in Jesus* have been reckoned righteous and therefore who can enter into communion with God. All other life is cut-flower life and is already evidently dying. 'If anyone is in Christ, he is a new creation' (2 Corinthians 5:17). So it is nothing less than a new creation (a new order of things) that Peter and John are proclaiming, and it is in that new order of things that the five thousand came to believe that day.

EXPERIENCE

Everything else, in so far as it did not contradict the new order of Jesus and the resurrection, stood in place. The temple could act as host mother for this cell of new life and so for a little while, until they were driven out, Solomon's Colonnade acted as a kind of meeting place for those interested in the new way. But you cannot in the end put new wine into old bottles: you cannot contain the champagne of this new life indefinitely, any more than Jesus could be contained by the tomb for more than three days. The Christians will soon flee the temple nest and the former things will pass away as God begins to do some new thing — the good news of the human race's possible destiny the other side of Jesus and the resurrection. 'As in Adam all die, so in Christ all will be made alive' (1 Corinthians 15:22).

It started in a sense with One Man on the cross at 3 pm on Good Friday in Jerusalem. Then twelve, five hundred, three thousand, five thousand — this thing is getting out of hand. Where on earth will it end?

But notice: faith is built on facts, however 'disturbing' those facts may be. We are not called just to have opinions.

The Chance to Change

The apostles performed many miraculous signs and wonders among the people. And all the believers used to meet together in Solomon's Colonnade. No one else dared join them, even though they were highly regarded by the people. Nevertheless, more and more men and women believed in the Lord and were added to their number. As a result, people brought the sick into the streets and laid them on beds and mats so that at least Peter's shadow might fall on some of them as he passed by. Crowds gathered also from the towns around Jerusalem, bringing their sick and those tormented by evil spirits, and all of them were healed.

Acts 5:12—16

'See you in Solomon's Colonnade!' seems to have been almost the password for the early Christians for a few weeks in the springtime of the first Pentecost. Solomon's Colonnade was one of the two great colonnades that surrounded the temple area. It had been a favourite loitering place for Jesus during his early ministry and now the body of Christ seemed to gravitate there in full public view, not ashamed to confess the same Jesus.

But notice two apparently conflicting dynamics in the witness of the early church. On the one hand, Luke tells us: 'No one else dared join them' even though 'they were highly regarded by the people.' Yet in the same breath Luke tells us that 'Nevertheless, more and more men and women believed in the Lord and were added to their number'. Here is a church which is the least exclusive gathering because it does not set out to be all-inclusive. You have to stand for something to be a member of the early church otherwise that early church would have fallen for anything. Being a Christian made a difference: there was something irresistible about such an appeal. Yet that appeal was not 'Come and join us' but rather 'Are you ready to be changed, to be healed and to be set free?' If you were not ready for that, then Christianity was not for you — at least, yet.

EXPLANATION

A gospel challenge which does not make demands will be by-passed by other more demanding challenges. Health clubs cannot be built fast enough to house all the neophytes of exercise and aerobics. Nevertheless such clubs certainly challenge people to the most rigorous routines and all this is done in the name of bodily health.

Yet in some sense the church is itself a health club. The word in Greek and Latin for salvation is the same as the word for health, at root. Indeed Tyndale in his first translation of the scriptures into English puts 'health' wherever we would put 'salvation'; in his later translations, 'physician' where we would 'Saviour' and 'healed' for where we would probably use the word 'saved'. That is what the apostles were offering in Solomon's Colonnade — health and therefore salvation. But remember the words of Jesus to the paralysed man at the pool of Bethesda 'Do you want to get well?' ('be healed' RSV John 5:6). So that is the line that has to be drawn and that is the line that you had to cross in Solomon's Colonnade if you wanted to join this new movement. If not, you had better remain where you are, standing on the edges of life, hiding in the shadows of the pillars and not getting caught up in all this new way of life.

EXPERIENCE

We probably fear change more than we fear death. Many people would rather die than change. The church does not exist so much to make good people better but rather to make bad people holy. Lives were touched and changed in Jerusalem in those first few weeks. People came out of the woodwork to declare for Christ — often the last people in the world you would ever have thought could or should become Christians!

'Men will always throng to a church where lives are changed,' says William Barclay. Does the church today evidently change people's lives, or do people strive to change the church in such a way that it no longer has the power to change anything? 'Do not be conformed to this world,' Paul insists in Romans 12, 'but be transformed by the renewal of your mind.' That is what those people experienced in Solomon's Colonnade — a renewal of their minds. 'The man who marries the spirit of this age will be a widower in the next,' warns Dean Inge. The church which would seek to change and evangelize the world soon experiences a kind of boomerang effect and discovers that it must first itself be changed and evangelized so that it does not conform so much to the world of the shadows but has the power to step out into the light of the kingdom of God. The early church was not accommodating: faith was not tailor-made but off-the-peg, take it or leave it. You would only be at home in that kind of gathering if you were ready to be changed, healed and therefore saved. A decade of evangelism will need to recover the full church's ministry of healing as it offers to the world the way of salvation.

So the question must be put again: is the church today that sort of church which expects change in the lives of its members? Whenever it is — wherever it is — such a church, lives indeed are changed and more and more men and women come 'to believe in the Lord' and are 'added to' the number of believers. Evangelism is very different from church growth. The former leads inevitably to the latter but to promote the latter for its own sake is to rob the world of the chance to change. Full-blooded evangelism is the most compassionate thing we have to offer the world today.

Feeding Minds or Washing Brains!

TUESDAY   **WEEK 5**

Now those who had been scattered by the persecution in connection with Stephen travelled as far as Phoenicia, Cyprus and Antioch, telling the message only to Jews. Some of them, however, men from Cyprus and Cyrene, went to Antioch and began to speak to Greeks also, telling them the good news about the Lord Jesus. The Lord's hand was with them, and a great number of people believed and turned to the Lord.

News of this reached the ears of the church at Jerusalem, and they sent Barnabas to Antioch. When he arrived and saw the evidence of the grace of God, he was glad and encouraged them all to remain true to the Lord with all their hearts. He was a good man, full of the Holy Spirit and faith, and a great number of people were brought to the Lord.

Then Barnabas went to Tarsus to look for Saul, and when he

found him, he brought him to Antioch. So for a whole year Barnabas and Saul met with the church and taught great numbers of people. The disciples were called Christians first at Antioch.

Acts 11:19—26

EVENT

Once you start letting converted Christians loose in the universe, there is no knowing where it all might end. Better still, if they are not just let loose, but rather driven out and dispersed to all sorts of corners and resting places where they would probably never choose to go, then the infection and contagion will really begin to spread. Of course it is no good just keeping them in quarantine. So the authorities could not in fact have done the church a better service than persecuting it and then scattering it abroad.

Some of those who were scattered only shared the message with fellow Jews of the Dispersion in Phoenicia (Lebanon), Cyprus and the cities of Syria and the Antioch region. But others simply could not contain themselves and they found themselves sharing the message of Jesus with Greeks and all-comers — especially in the very cosmopolitan city of Antioch. After Jerusalem and Rome it was the next best, strategic city to tackle. Founded in 300 BC by Seleucus Nicator, he named it Antioch after his father Antiochus, and its nearby port he named Seleucia, after himself. It had a great international reputation as a fine city. Nicknamed Antioch the Beautiful, with its grand buildings, it had fine, long and well-paved boulevards running from north to south with spacious colonnades, having trees and fountains on either side. With a total population of nearly half a million in the first century, in addition to its large colony of Jews it also housed people from as far as India, China and Persia, because of whom this fine city was also known as the Queen of the East. It was the capital city of the Roman province of Syria and so it also had a sizeable population of Romans and came to be regarded by the Jewish historian, Josephus, as 'the third city of the empire'.

Barnabas now went to Tarsus to reclaim for the church, seven years or so after his conversion, Paul, who had spent that time reconstructing his faith around the person of Christ as the fulfilment of the old religion and as the pioneer of the new. Barnabas had spotted Paul as having just that kind of mind that was needed to work out a theology that would keep pace with the missionary church as it exploded out of the confines of Judaism into the Gentile world. Barnabas, in his pragmatic and large-hearted way, was under no illusions about the catholicity of the missionary vision. By nature and by name he was a man of encouragement — *largesse du coeur*. When he had arrived in Antioch he had seen for himself 'the evidence of the grace of God' at work and by his patient goodness many people would be brought to the Lord Jesus, whom Barnabas commended by his sheer love and presence. However Barnabas was big enough to know his limitations. He needed a good mind in Antioch to work with him at the Christian institute: to teach as well as to preach and to begin serious Christian education as well as evangelism. The two needed to go hand in hand. They still do.

A call to evangelism must be a call to serious commitment to Christian education and formation. We need to praise God, Paul tells us, with both the mind and the heart (1 Corinthians 14:15). Barnabas, Barclay tells us, was 'the man with the biggest heart in the church'. But world-wide mission in various cultures needed also a man with what Justin Martyr used to call 'a flame in the mind' to convince as well as to convert these large numbers of Gentile enquirers who were flooding into the Christian institute in the fine capital city of Antioch. Only so would a great number of people be brought in heart and mind to the Lord and not to some new hypnotic superstition or hysterical new enthusiasm. It was not just a question of brain-washing, but mind-feeding that was needed.

Our church today needs both Pauls and Barnabasses. It needs a robust educational strategy, targeted to many different people of all ages from different backgrounds and cultures — who will not become members of a sect or cult of the mediaeval western Way, but who will take their place in the catholic church of Jesus Christ as critical Christians from every race, colour and tongue. Then we can with humility and gratitude claim in some sense to 'have the mind of Christ' (1 Corinthians 2:16). The whole church needs to go back to school, to learn a reason for the hope that is in us and to equip us to withstand the brainwashing of our contemporary world — not least in the supermarket of religious and superstitious options which are multiplying so rapidly as we appraoch the millennial hysteria of AD 2000. Minds need feeding, otherwise brains will be washed, and of course all in the name of new-age religion! The world needs a message not just a massage!

A Message or A Massage?

Then Paul and Barnabas answered them boldly: 'We had to speak the word of God to you first. Since you reject it and do not consider yourselves worthy of eternal life, we now turn to the Gentiles. For this is what the Lord has commanded us:

"I have made you a light for the Gentiles,

that you may bring salvation to the ends of the earth."

When the Gentiles heard this, they were glad and honoured the word of the Lord; and all who were appointed for eternal life believed.

The word of the Lord spread through the whole region. But the Jews incited the God-fearing women of high standing and the leading men of the city. They stirred up persecution against Paul and Barnabas, and expelled them from their region. So they shook the dust from their feet in protest against them and went to Iconium. And the disciples were filled with joy and with the Holy Spirit.

Acts 13:46—52

EVENT

Notice what Luke tells us is spreading: the word of the Lord. The Gentiles are glad and are honouring the word of the Lord. At the same time, the word of the Lord was spreading 'through the whole region'. Indeed the picture painted of Paul and Barnabas' ministry in Antioch was so fruitful that Luke may have been somewhat carried away with his description of the local response to the word of the Lord when he tells us that 'on the next Sabbath, the whole city . . . gathered'. Notice that once again they gathered to hear 'the word of the Lord': a message with power.

Furthermore, we need to notice that 'the disciples were filled with joy and with the Holy Spirit'. For that word was an anointed word and it spread like wildfire. Yet if the word of the Lord is powerfully anointed, not only is it received, but it is also rejected. Yet the tragedy of Antioch is the same as we have seen elsewhere: the 'outsiders' received that word with joy (Gentiles) while the 'insiders' (Jews) reject it. The question we need to ask, before any evangelization endeavour, is essentially: 'Do we want this church to grow?'

EXPLANATION

Notice the strategy of the opposition. 'When the Jews saw the crowds, they were filled with jealousy . . .' Often the local ministry is jealous of the response elicited by the visiting evangelists — especially when they see 'the crowds'. Contrast the Jews filled with jealousy with the disciples who are filled with joy. Of course if you think in terms of successful evangelism and see evangelization as

---

the work of human skill and talent, then pride will be your response to large crowds, and jealousy your response to large crowds when they listen to another preacher. If of course you see evangelization as the spreading of the 'word of the Lord', through the anointing and gift of the Holy Spirit, then joy will fill you when you see crowds receiving that same word of life which originally touched your life, and this will be true even if this ends up with you being put out of a job: with one of those 'new' people making the coffee next Sunday, reading the lessons, giving the chalice or suddenly in the limelight . . . So again the question: 'Do we really want crowds of *new* people in *our* church next week?'

EXPERIENCE

Because, you see, the arrangements in the local synagogue until the previous Sabbath had suited everybody very nicely — then Paul and Barnabas started to disturb things. 'The God-fearing women of high standing' found in the teaching of the Jewish religion that their status in decadent Roman society was much more protected. 'Round the synagogues gathered men and women, often of high social position, who found in this teaching (Jewish teaching) just what they longed for' (William Barclay). The local synagogue at Antioch was full of such women, who were often married to the leading men of the city. They had built for themselves in the name of religion a powerful and influential club — a somewhat self-selective club at that, which offered them just the kind of massage they needed and wanted. Now here come Paul and Barnabas, opening the doors of the synagogue wide and inviting the 'whole city' (irrespective of race, religion, colour or social standing) to hear 'the word of the Lord'. These people must be got rid of, quickly before things really get out of hand!

Are we a church that is really ready to be turned upside down by new members? For the bald truth is inescapable: there can be no new Christians from the outside coming inside, unless the old Christians inside are renewed and prepared to welcome gladly the outsiders — into the fellowship of a church which is the Lord's church and not theirs. Is our church half-empty or half-full? Is there room for the word of the Lord in our church? Does our church preach a revolutionary message to insiders and outsiders alike, or do we simply offer a supportive massage to carefully chosen customers? Openness to new Christians from the outside will demand that the Christians on the inside are ready to be renewed. The church needs to be renewed for evangelism: renewal and evangelization need to go hand-in-hand.

Altitude or Attitude

After he said this, he was taken up before their very eyes, and a cloud hid him from their sight.

They were looking intently up into the sky as he was going, when suddenly two men dressed in white stood beside them. 'Men of Galilee,' they said, 'why do you stand here looking into the sky? This same Jesus, who has been taken from you into heaven, will come back in the same way you have seen him go into heaven.'

Then they returned to Jerusalem from the hill called the Mount of Olives, a Sabbath day's walk from the city.

Acts 1:9—12

EVENT

'In our end is our beginning' (T.S. Eliot). The ascension of Jesus marks the end of a chapter one in Jesus' earthly ministry and also the beginning of chapter two. Yet notice that both chapters are very down-to-earth. They are the gospel and Acts accounts of Jesus' earthly ministry. In chapter one that earthly ministry is through the physical body of Jesus of Nazareth anointed throughout with the Holy Spirit. Necessarily, that ministry is limited in terms of time and space and it is tied to the whereabouts of the physical person of Jesus at any one moment. In chapter two (Acts) that same earthly ministry of the heavenly Jesus Christ is through the sacramental body of Christ, anointed at baptism — the church, increasingly unlimited in terms of time and space. However, that body of Jesus is still tied to the whereabouts of the members of the body of Christ. To put it more accurately still, both chapter one and chapter two (before and after the ascension) are about the work of God the Father, through the body of Jesus (earthly in chapter one, sacramental in chapter two) anointed by the same Holy Spirit. Both chapter one and two are the work of the blessed Trinity, doing the will of God 'on earth as it is in heaven' — going out of its way in the name of love. We call it mission.

So although we draw a line, as Luke does, beginnings and endings, we must be careful not to divide in wrong ways what belongs to one unified, single-minded activity. 'God (all three Persons) so loved the world . . .' (John 3:16) — that is the simple message of both the gospel of Luke and the book of Acts. The message, the Messenger and the method are one and the same throughout: it is God working in and through all things. Both the gospel and the book of Acts are a continuing record of what happens in the real presence of Jesus (whether bodily or sacramentally) as, anointed by the Holy Spirit, he seeks to do the will of the Father.

EXPLANATION

The line of the ascension is a line drawn between two different kinds of presence: physical presence and sacramental presence. The only way we know how to draw a line around presence of course is to talk about its opposite — namely, absence. This is the theological significance of the ascension which is much more important than any geographical significance. Put another way: the ascension of Jesus is more to do with attitude than with altitude.

'Won't it be heavenly in heaven?' No, not if you have the wrong attitude — it will be hell! Heaven is that state or place where Jesus is truly present and where we are seeking to do the will of the Father by the power of the Holy Spirit. The proper attitude is summed up in one word, *amen. Fiat mihi* (Let it be to me . . .) — when Mary said that word by the power of the Holy Spirit, for a moment it was heaven on earth! So the line we need to draw is not a line of space, nor is it concerned primarily with altitude. It is the line which is most certainly there but it is a line we cross over when *we are moved* to do the will of the Father in the real presence of Jesus by the power of the Holy Spirit. Then for a moment it is heavenly on earth, in space, in time — even in Galilee.

EXPERIENCE

The church at worship week by week is intended to move across that line in the liturgy. 'Lift up your hearts' — not so much a question of altitude as attitude. 'They are with the Lord,' we reply. The whole body of the faithful at that moment of the great amen at the conclusion of the Prayer of Thanksgiving and with the words of the prayer of the kingdom on our lips (Our Father) — at that moment, priest and people are together moved over into the kingdom, for a moment we are all enkingdomed and presented to the Father in heaven. As the body of Christ is lifted up, Holy Spirit comes down (though remember, altitude is not our prime concern). Pentecost follows hard on the heels of the ascension as the gifts of the ascended Christ are given to his church to empower for ministry and mission. And the work of that church, in a single word, is always to make Jesus truly present — to represent him and to re-present him.

That is the challenge then of the feast of the Ascension — namely, not to be so heavenly minded as to be no earthly use, but rather to be willing to experience the absence of Jesus in one dimension (spacial, altitude, etc.) in order to receive him fully present in another way (universally and sacramentally — new attitudes). So 'there was something fundamentally anomalous about their gazing up into the sky,' writes John Stott, 'when they had been commissioned to go to the ends of the earth. It was the earth not the sky which was to be their preoccupation. Their calling was to be witnesses, not star-gazers.'

And so is ours: witnesses who bring the real presence of the heavenly Christ down to earth — and all of that, every week, Sunday by Sunday, in every parish church.

Establishing Growth

They preached the good news in [Derbe] and won a large number of disciples. Then they returned to Lystra, Iconium and Antioch, strengthening the disciples and encouraging them to remain true to the faith. 'We must go through many hardships to enter the kingdom of God,' they said. Paul and Barnabas appointed elders for them in each church and, with prayer and fasting, committed them to the Lord, in whom they had put their trust. After going through Pisidia, they came into Pamphylia, and when they had preached the word in Perga, they went down to Attalia.

From Attalia they sailed back to Antioch, where they had been committed to the grace of God for the work they had now completed. On arriving there, they gathered the church together and reported all that God had done through them and how he had opened the door of faith to the Gentiles. And they stayed there a long time with the disciples.

Acts 14:21—28

'Nothing can alter or disguise the fact that St Paul did leave behind him at his first visit complete churches,' writes the well-known missionologist, Roland Allen. These churches were indigenous, local, self-supporting, self-governing and therefore self-extending. They were planted in such a way that they could grow. In a single decade of evangelism, AD 47 to 57, 'Paul established churches in four provinces of the empire — Galatia, Macedonia, Achea and Asia.'

We need to learn from that 47—57 decade of evangelization, to equip us for the decade of evangelism faced by all the churches at the conclusion of the second millennium. Space does not permit a sufficiently detailed analysis of Paul's strategy, but we would do well to take this passage and learn from its contents.

EXPLANATION

In the first place there was follow-up to this initial evangelism programme. The apostolic band returned to Lystra, Iconium and Antioch with an expressed purpose of 'strengthening the disciples and encouraging them in the faith'. It would seem that even as early as AD 50 there was an agreed and recognizable body of essential, saving doctrine which constituted a tradition or a deposit of faith and teaching. The apostle embodied that teaching and was in himself a walking tradition. You could undertake an interesting exercise, as many scholars have done, by reconstructing the essential ingredients of that tradition from the New Testament epistles and you would end up with a sketchy outline of what later came to be known as the creeds of the church — signposts for disciples and mandates for the new baptised. Apostolic teaching was a living, dynamic tradition, crossing and recrossing Asia Minor and the Mediterranean world. By the middle of the first century it was universal, not merely local and it shunned the eccentric.

Then we read that 'Paul and Barnabas appointed elders for them,' in each of the churches. Notice that there was more than one elder to a church. Jesus had sent them out two by two. Paul never worked alone, but rather in tandem with colleagues and companions such as Mark, Silas, Timothy, Barnabas, Luke or others from the Pauline circle. Generally there was a woman on the team, Priscilla or Lydia. In other words, each of the local churches would have a local, indigenous pastoral team exercising oversight while being at the same time related to the wider apostolic ministry. Nevertheless the church was essentially local — speaking in the language of the culture and region. The relation of the local ministry to the wider apostolic ministry ensured that the church was at one and the same time both local and universal, indigenous yet catholic.

There is a final ingredient which is essential if the church is to grow and expand and not remain dependent. We are told that Barnabas and Paul, after prayer, committed those fragile, infant churches 'to the Lord in whom they had put their trust'.

There was nothing paternalistic about Paul and Barnabas' ministry: they did not rush around Asia Minor creating dependencies. Why was that? The answer is simple. They knew that it was God's church, that mission is the work of God and that God can be trusted to take care of his people. Hence those churches were free to grow and Antioch became one of the great centres of Christianity with many other churches clustered and scattered around it. Once the churches grew too large, as in a good garden, they would split and another congregation would be planted, take root, raise up elders and a local ministry, multiplying and splitting again. All of it was the Lord's doing and was entrusted in the last resort to him.

EXPERIENCE

However, much of the missionary activity of the church, especially in the eighteenth and nineteenth centuries, has not followed this pattern of St Paul and the early church. Instead, we encouraged dependencies — the church in America was to have episcopal oversight from London and be ruled like any other colony from Westminster! Little wonder Anglicanism got off on such a bad start in the United States. Then the new churches worshipped and the gospel was packaged in the clothes of British imperialism, and missionary work was seen eventually as supporting the gospel wrapped in Victorian externals, ministering from strength to weakness in the style of benevolent paternalism, accompanied by harmoniums and instructed by archdeacons in gaiters.

Dame Julian, looking at the small hazel nut in her hand observed three things about that: 'God made it; God loved it; and God could take care of it.' All three observations are equally true of Christ's expanding church. If we are to engage in an evangelism which is free to grow and expand, we need to know and recall all three of those observations in relation to the spread of the church today.

Don't Rock The Boat!

When he came to Jerusalem, he tried to join the disciples, but they were all afraid of him, not believing that he really was a disciple. But Barnabas took him and brought him to the apostles. he told them how Saul on his journey had seen the Lord and that the Lord had spoken to him, and how in Damascus he had preached fearlessly in the name of Jesus. So Saul stayed with them and moved about freely in Jerusalem, speaking boldly in the name of the Lord. He talked and debated with the Grecian Jews, but they tried to kill him. When the brothers learned of this, they took him down to Caesarea and sent him off to Tarsus.

Then the church throughout Judea, Galilee and Samaria enjoyed a time of peace. It was strengthened; and encouraged by the Holy Spirit, it grew in numbers, living in the fear of the Lord.

Acts 9:26—31

Was the church ready for new converts — especially the sort that were going to rock the boat? Did they really believe that grace and gospel could really change people's lives: 'that "wolves" could become "sheep"', to use Calvin's own description of Paul's conversion? After all Paul constituted a real risk for the early church. Of course it was just possible that Paul had really been converted, but was it not just as credible to believe that he was planted as a spy? It is important to remember that Paul would spend the rest of his life bumping into relatives and friends of people (like Stephen) in whose persecution or martyrdom he as Saul of Tarsus had been involved. It is not too much to suppose that close relatives and friends of Stephen's were members of the church either at Damascus or Jerusalem, and now, here he is, Saul of Tarsus at the same communion table with Stephen's mother, cousin or closest friend. It took a bit of swallowing!

So Barnabas takes Paul and introduces him to the apostles, speaking on Paul's behalf of the contradiction of conversion. Clearly these verses suggest that Paul's presence in Jerusalem was deeply disturbing not only to the Jewish community and to the Grecian Jews, but also not a little to the community of faith. It would seem that when Paul finally left Jerusalem (aided by the well-intentioned Christians), it was 'then' (verse 31) that the church enjoyed a time of peace. The church has always been a little embarrassed by its new converts. It has preferred its role as a luxury liner to that of a lifeboat.

For it is the new convert with all the enthusiasm and zeal of that conversion who reminds the church and recalls the church to its true identity. So often it is those who are rowing the boat who resent most those who certainly rock the boat as they climb aboard. Yet, 'I came,' says Jesus, 'not to call the righteous, but sinners to repentance' (Luke 5:32). The church exists for the sake of those who are not members of it. The ninety-nine exist for the sake of the one. The only moderating factor in all of this is that the minute the one becomes a member of the niney-nine, then he or she exists now for another one who is still outside, over the edge, struggling to get out of the waves and into the boat. Notice that Saul moves over from being the persecutor to being the persecuted. We are saved, to save others — 'He saved others, himself he cannot save,' was said with irony of the Christ, and it is equally applicable, with even more irony, to those who seek to follow him.

EXPERIENCE

Is our local congregation ready for and expectant of the most unlikely converts coming through its doors next Sunday? Have we appointed an Ananias or Barnabas to have one eye always ready and open to receive and introduce such folk to the fellowship of the church? Is the local congregation sufficiently open to receive — warmly — a recovering alcoholic, people who are suffering from Aids, or the tragic casualties of drug abuse? Converts will rock the boat, but we need to remember that the boat is a lifeboat before it is a luxury liner: a school for sinners before it is a home for saints.

Notice that the only fear that was characteristic of the early, expanding church was the fear of the Lord. 'Fear him ye saints, and you will then have nothing else to fear.' They did not fear what people were saying or the possibility of persecution. They grew in numbers, because they grew in godliness — 'strengthened and encouraged by the Holy Spirit'. If the church, like Jesus its master, is to associate with sinners, prostitutes, the sick and those of bad reputation, inevitably people will speak ill of us. The Lord does not always give us respectable converts and often the world will have a bad word to say about new converts who have formerly been notorious sinners and leaders in the world's corridors of power. They will think they are frauds, cashing in on religion. They may well be so. Little wonder that they raise their eyebrows. But for those of us who are members of the household of faith, who know both the 'scriptures and the power of God' (Mark 12:24) and who have experienced the grace of God at work in our lives, it should be a different matter. We should be familiar with the story of sinners who have become saints — Sauls who became Pauls.

Try standing in front of a large cathedral. Many European examples have stood in their splendid magnificence for nearly one thousand years. Now start to make the connection: the essential connection. Those stones are standing there because once upon a time one stone was removed from the entrance to one tomb. The resurrection of Jesus not only moved that one huge stone which had been rolled across the entrance to the sepulchre, but it has continued to move stones ever since, constructing thousands of glorious buildings in every continent of the world — and all of them standing as concrete evidence for Jesus and the resurrection.

But there is a further connection to make as we reflect upon the concrete reality of the church — a connection which is even more telling. 'You also, like living stones, are being built into a spiritual house . . .' (1 Peter 2:5). Christianity — the most rapidly growing religion in the world today — is not an idea or a movement, but a *body* of men and women through whose lives this same Jesus gains entry into our concrete everyday world. The church, if you like, is God's skin in flesh-and-blood terms.

The only qualification to be a member of that body is the genuine desire to be one. The church is not a self-selecting group like a tennis club — you can always keep 'undesirables' out of those kind of bodies. But anybody can be a member of the body of Christ — which is why there are so many bad Christians in the world today; there always have been. You do not qualify to be a Christian and no one experience, however transcendent or deeply religious, makes you a Christian. Only baptism by water and the Spirit makes you a Christian and a member of this body which we call the church. Of course it can make you a bad Christian, or rather an indifferent Christian. It is certainly a lifetime's job to become a good or holy Christian. Perfectionism will tempt people to wait until they can do it well before they are ever baptised. That is not the Christian, catholic answer, however. The prodigal son was a bad son — and probably always would be a bit of a problem child, yet the point of the story is that he is a son and not a slave. He is a bad son — not half so 'good' as his elder brother. Nevertheless he was a son, and the sooner he realized that and stopped all that business about endless self-justification as a servant running round the house to assuage his guilt, the sooner everybody would be happier. He would have loved to have spent the rest of his life working off the guilt of those years when he had squandered his father's goods. What a miserable place he would have made that home! But no, the father is adamant from the moment he returns — he is a son.

Hence the need in evangelism for an altar call — an opportunity for those who feel so moved to come forward and to re-affirm and to express for the first time the moving experience of their faith. The church is the community of those who express a moving experience by stepping out and coming forward to opt for Christ: stand up stand up for Jesus! *Ecclesia* — the Latin word for church — means just that — to be called out. In many ways, the church is the community of displaced people — folk who have been moved from complacency to confession, conversion and commitment.

For God refuses to draw lines between first, second or third class Christians — all alike are Christ's people, the good, the bad and the indifferent. The only line there is in the line of baptism — significantly water, a river or a sea, dividing the shadowlands from the promised land. God's Red Sea people — in Old and New Testaments alike — have all been 'through it'. They have undergone baptism as an outward and visible expression of an inward movement of heart and will.

So the church is itself a sacrament: an outward, visible and tangible sign in stones (living and otherwise), in flesh and blood — of the inner movement of the Spirit.

Yet we must notice that the church is formed and reformed by the gospel and by the power of the gospel. We must not substitute the church for the gospel and we certainly must not substitute the church for the kingdom. To do that would be to fob people off with churchianity rather than Christianity. The gospel and the catholic church belong together — but the church must never degenerate simply into an organization for propagating some ideas about Jesus of Nazareth. It must essentially remain a body with all the reality of flesh and blood.

By the overshadowing of the Holy Spirit, the church is a sign of the real presence of Jesus — through word, worship and life in the Spirit. It is one miracle to believe that the Jesus of Nazareth who walked the streets of Palestine was truly and physically the body of Christ. It is another miracle to believe that the sacrament on the altar, week by week, is the sacramental body of Christ. But perhaps the greatest miracle of all three is the realization that each and every week at thousands of altars all over the world, gathered into one fellowship and mystical union, is the mystical body of Christ. Tom, John, Mary and Sally are the body of Christ — the outward and visible expression in flesh-and-blood terms of the message of the gospel and the real presence of the Messenger in our town and community, as surely as Jesus was present when he came into Galilee preaching the good news of the kingdom nearly two thousand years ago.

Questions for reflection during the week and for discussion in the group

1. In what practical and concrete ways does the church throughout its history prove that the death and resurrection of Jesus is an eternally true fact?
2. Why is it so difficult to be a member of the church?
    Why have Christians fought each other so much throughout their history?
3. In the conclusion of chapter two in Acts (from verse 42 on), Luke gives us a thumbnail sketch of what the early church looked like. What is on that list which is missing in a similar list which an observer would draw up from life in your local church?
4. Is Confirmation the best time to receive people for Holy Communion? What about infant baptism and therefore infant Communion?

A Cell of New Life

Then they returned to Jerusalem from the hill called the Mount of Olives, a Sabbath day's walk from the city. When they arrived, they went upstairs to the room where they were staying. Those present were Peter, John, James and Andrew; Philip and Thomas, Bartholomew and Matthew; James son of Alphaeus and Simon the Zealot, and Judas son of James. They all joined together constantly in prayer, along with the women and Mary the mother of Jesus, and with his brothers.

Acts 1:12—14

EVENT

The church is the expression of the gospel in time, space and history with an address and a telephone number, because, as we have said before, Christianity is not an idea; Christianity is not any *thing*, it is some*body*: it is the body of Christ.

So we notice several distinctive characteristics among this band of disciples. Luke tells us that they constituted in total about one hundred and twenty believers (verse 15), who had in some sense been caught in the whole event of the death and resurrection of Jesus. They were both women as well as men (as listed here specifically by Luke). A distinctive constituent of the larger number were the eleven apostles — the twelfth being added after prayer and the drawing of lots.

That little cell was pregnant with expectation, waiting for the fulfilment of the promises of Jesus and poised on the edge of world-wide mission. That was the small acorn from which the huge catholic oak tree of the church has grown. Small is beautiful and for Christians we can say as we look back over the history of the church — small is bountiful; grace is sufficient.

It started with one hundred and twenty people. What was their plan and their agenda? They did not have a plan, but they did follow a practice and then the plan emerged from daily practice — their way of life.

In the first place, they continued in their commitment to worship and praise in the temple, *continually*. Straight away on their return from the Mount of Olives (about half a mile away) they went to that upper room, and *constantly* joined together in prayer. From the outset the believers formed a closely related body, identifying with Jesus of Nazareth. That body included both those who were related to Jesus and to each other by blood (his mother and brothers), and those who were related to each other by grace and commitment to that same Jesus — all of them, Luke tells us, 'joined together constantly in prayer'.

The word Luke uses for 'together' in Greek is one of his very favourite words. Although in the whole of the New Testament this word occurs only once from the pens of all the other writers put together, it occurs no less than ten times in the writings of Luke. For Luke, one of the prime characteristics of the church of Jesus Christ was its togetherness. In that sense, while of course the church was to become unbelievably diverse in colour, race and culture, it was at the same time quite remarkably together in its common life. The church for Luke was essentially catholic and cosmopolitan yet at the same time it was of one mind and heart in its purposes, objectives and life together. When the church comes together to pray, the devil trembles. He is much happier when these Christians copy the world and strive to do their own thing! He always divides to rule.

Evangelism must necessarily be ecumenical, yet ecumenical in that fuller sense than we have tended to use that word in the past. We must not try to come up first with an agreed plan and then pray that God will put his signature to our agreed statement for unity. Rather, it must be the other way round. We must come together in prayer, praise and worship. When we do so we must bring all of what we are, with our rich and yet diverse practices of worship and praise. Christian unity is not a smorgasbord, a little of this and a little of that and everything in moderation with nothing that will upset the body. No it is not a smorgasbord, but a casserole. The recipe permits and positively encourages us to throw in everything which has proved over the years to be powerful for the gospel. Let the Baptists bring their preaching and the Roman Catholics their discipline of the sacramental life; throw this in with transcendent worship in the communion of saints that we find in Eastern Orthodoxy. Let the Evangelicals practise their altar call and the Pentecostalists their intoxicating prayer and praise. (Perhaps the Anglicans can teach us how to dress and to worship in an orderly fashion!) Then the Salvationists will insist on taking us out into the streets for our witness and Mother Teresa along with St Francis will have no time for us unless we have a passion for the poor and needy.

'Let everything that hath breath praise the Lord.' So let everything that has divided us and fed party spirit, be subsumed in the rich catholic casserole of an evangelistic church 'joined constantly in prayer'. Nothing less will win the multicultural world for the catholic Christ.

That band of one hundred and twenty already hold the essential marks of the church — holy (in prayer), catholic (in diversity), apostolic (with the twelve) but *one* in constant prayer and praise. What about the church today?

What Sort of Church?

They devoted themselves to the apostles' teaching and to the fellowship, to the breaking of bread and to prayer. Everyone was filled with awe, and many wonders and miraculous signs were done by the apostles. All the believers were together and had everything in common. Selling their possessions and goods, they gave to anyone as he had need. Every day they continued to meet together in the temple courts. They broke bread in their homes and ate together with glad and sincere hearts, praising God and enjoying the favour of all the people. And the Lord added to their number daily those who were being saved.

Acts 2:42—47

EVENT

Every so often, through the book of Acts, Luke gives a kind of summary and progress report on how things were going. The book of Acts has a real sense of purpose and direction. This section at the end of chapter two is the first of six or seven such reports and summaries about the growing life of the church (6:7; 9:31; 12:24; 16:5; 19:20; 28:31). In this first summary, Luke gives us a list of ingredients and characteristics as he observed them in the formation of what, with hindsight, we have come to call one, holy, catholic and apostolic church. Yet there is nothing self-conscious about the early church: there is no clericalism or ecclesiasticism. 'They did not think of the church as a kind of thing in itself,' says Michael Ramsey. 'They were concerned only with the dying and rising of Jesus and the power of his death and resurrection at work in their lives.' They were totally free in other words of ecclesiasticism!

So the church slowly emerged. The word of God under the Spirit of God formed and reformed the people of God into the church of God. The church is the visible, tangible, continuing evidence in history that Jesus really was raised from the dead; that he is alive and that he reigns. The features of the church should reflect the features of the gospel, not as an idea but as a record in flesh and blood of the power of the gospel to make a difference in the lives of everyday people.

EXPERIENCE

So what difference does the gospel make? We observe several signs of spiritual renewal in Luke's first summary.

1. It was a learning church. Apostolic doctrine or the teaching programme of the apostles was given pride of place. In that programme of education and Christian formation they sought to learn the mind of Christ. There was nothing mindless about life in the Spirit, for he is not only the spirit of love and joy, he is also the spirit of truth and Jesus promises that he will lead faithful Christian disciples into all truth.

2. It was a church of love and fellowship. 'There went with him (King Saul) a band of men whose hearts God had touched' (1 Samuel 10:26). Jesus had said that the best evidence that a group of disciples were truly Christian and disciples of Jesus Christ was that they 'loved one another' (John 15:12, 17). That is evidence which impresses the world — and distresses the world, when they see the opposite in a church or congregation.

3. It was a worshipping church not only in the formality of the temple but in the informality of people's houses. We need both structure and formality in the full life of the church, together with spontaneity and informality. The two opposites belong together. As the Jews in the Old Testament had at least three dimensions in their worship — family, synagogue and temple, so as Christians we need at least three similar dimensions in our worship today: cell,

congregation, cathedral. Each has its own proper and appropriate place. Worship and prayer can be informal but must never be trivial — there must be a proper sense of reverence and awe (verse 43).

4. It was a church of event where things happened — 'signs and wonders'. They expected that a lively faith would make a difference to everyday life — sometimes a dramatic difference, as in the case of the blind beggar or as in the prophecy from the Old Testament: the blind begin to see, the deaf begin to hear and the lame begin to leap (Isaiah 35).

5. It was a sharing and a caring church, where some people from time to time would sell their possessions and share their resources. It was a community of faith, which is not the same thing as saying that it was Communist. The church of God, as it partakes of communion with God, is soon fashioned into the life of the community who is the blessed Trinity. Love is communion and can begin to express itself in and through true community. God reveals the very nature of his own life in the daily life of his church, and it is a life of community and communion.

6. It was a celebrating church, full of joy, that fruit of the Spirit which is second only to love. Therefore inevitably (chapter 8) an evangelistic church. Here again there was nothing self-conscious or calculating about this evangelism. It was an inevitable by-product of being truly the church of Jesus Christ. Furthermore, God was the prime evangelist, adding those who were being saved to the church in each and every day. Notice that people did not join — this is not a question of church growth. They were added, as they were being saved, to the community of salvation. Salvation and the church belong together like 'love and marriage', 'horse and carriage' and all the other duets of real life.

We might want to go down this check list and measure it against the life, features and characteristics of our local congregation.

A Witnessing Church

Then they called them in again and commanded them not to speak or teach at all in the name of Jesus. But Peter and John replied, 'Judge for yourselves whether it is right in God's sight to obey you rather than God. For we cannot help speaking about what we have seen and heard.'

After further threats they let them go. They could not decide how to punish them, because all the people were praising God for what had happened. For the man who was miraculously healed was over forty years old.

Acts 4:18—22

EVENT

Christianity is not primarily concerned with weighing different opinions — because it is primarily committed to interpreting facts. It is no accident that the central word in the vocabulary of Christian proclamation is the central word in the vocabulary of the court room: witness. The job of the defending and prosecuting counsel alike is to establish the facts and to that end they call upon witnesses. The Bible is not full of visions, dreams and ecstatic experiences. Rather, it is a record of events, facts and acts — apostolic acts.

So with the witnessing of Peter and John. There is not much that the Sanhedrin can do, while the embarrassing evidence of the miraculously healed man is standing there for all to see. Like the empty tomb or the healed man born blind in John's gospel, there is need to dispose of this embarrassing evidence so that it can be explained some other way. To witness, therefore, in the New Testament is not to parade your opinions in front of people, but rather to tell the story and present the facts of the case — to give your evidence.

As Lesslie Newbigin points out so well in his book, *The Gospel in a Pluralist Society*, the twentieth century is rightly willing to be pluralist in matters of opinion, but is still (and rightly) dogmatic about facts and figures — especially in the realm of scientific evidence. The big mistake of our age is we have lumped Christianity with opinions, feelings, intuitions; and then we have gone on to proclaim that everyone on matters of religion of that kind is entitled to their own opinion — thus encouraging pluralism in religion. That may be all right for all religions other than Judaistic Christianity. Christianity stands out like a sore thumb among all other world religions. For Christianity is essentially an historical religion based on facts, with a story to tell. Christianity does not belong in the religious basket at all: it should be placed in with the scientific disciplines which are based primarily upon the evidence of facts about a universe in which there are some embarrassing factors. For if we were to tell the full story we would have to admit that somebody has risen from the dead somewhere, sometime in history. We might want to go on and conclude therefore that there is a distinct possibility that we shall be needing to reinterpret the facts of the universe, leaving room for the impossible. We might even want to go further and rebuild our structure of the universe upon this one contradictory fact — someone has risen from the dead somewhere. Resurrection is part of the reality which all are called upon to scrutinize. The case for the resurrection of Jesus does not stand or fall therefore upon opinion or upon my existential, personal experience. Either it is a fact or a fiction — and faith is built not on the latter but on the former. Faith is the fact which makes the most sense of all the facts.

Witnessing therefore is simply a matter of telling your story: it is history coming alive in the first person. There is a sense in which we 'cannot help speaking about what we have seen and heard'. For far from being inappropriate at a dinner party, people's stories make for the best dinner-table talk. You may wish to rule out sex, politics and religion as inappropriate table talk — but Christianity is not in that sense a religion. The compulsive popularity of soap operas is no accident, for there is nothing which makes for more compulsive listening and gains our attention more fully than when some one insists upon telling of something that has happened to them.

In those early days all of the church, not only the apostles, but also every baptised Christian in Jerusalem was busy gossiping the gospel.

In Alcoholics Anonymous, you tell your story. After a while the inquirer or neophyte begins to realize that in some way that is his or her story. The story is not an opinion about alcohol or alcoholics. Rather is a story based on facts — what happened or what you have seen and heard and experienced. That is what people need to hear and that is what all baptised Christians need to tell. As God's Red Sea people we need to remember, recall and relate what we have been through, telling and retelling the story of what the Lord has done for our souls — as we do on Easter Eve at the vigil service. It is by telling our story that we recover and uncover our identity.

So the creeds of the catholic church are not a long list of opinions about this or that, but rather they are based on the record of a God who has made himself known to us by what he has done for us — through the virgin Mary; under Pontius Pilate; once upon a time; in time to change the shape of all times to the end of time and beyond.

We say the creeds, but better still we sing them — and you cannot sing opinions.

As the catholic church continues to gossip the gospel in every generation, fresh evidence comes to light. The resurrection which happened once upon a time somewhere is continuing to happen all the time everywhere — even to lame men of forty — and so the story goes on. There is no way that you could suppress these witnesses, for in the end the truth will out; and if the whole story were told, 'I suppose that even the whole world would not have room for the books that would be written' (John 21:25).

A Church With The Right Priorities

In those days when the number of disciples was increasing, the Grecian Jews among them complained against the Hebraic Jews because their widows were being overlooked in the daily distribution of food. So the Twelve gathered all the disciples together and said, 'It would not be right for us to neglect the ministry of the word of God in order to wait on tables. Brothers, choose seven men from among you who are known to be full of the Spirit and wisdom. We will turn this responsibility over to them and will give our attention to prayer and the ministry of the word.'

This proposal pleased the whole group. They chose Stephen, a man full of faith and of the Holy Spirit; also Philip, Procorus, Nicanor, Timon, Parmenas, and Nicolas from Antioch, a convert to Judaism. They presented these men to the apostles, who prayed and laid their hands on them.

Acts 6:1—6

EVENT

There were two kinds of Jewish Christians emerging in Jerusalem. On the one hand there were the Palestinian and Jerusalem Jews, who spoke Aramaic and had not forgotten their Hebrew. This group would tend to pride itself on having purely Jewish roots, never having left Palestine. Then there were the Jews who had come back to Palestine, after living for several generations (perhaps) in foreign countries as part of the Dispersion, where they had spoken Greek and lost touch with their Hebrew-speaking roots. 'The natural consequence,' writes William Barclay, 'was that the spiritually snobbish Aramaic-speaking Jews looked down on the foreign Jews.'

Not unnaturally, Aramaic-speaking Jews continued to expect the routine custom of the synagogue to apply in the life of the church. In the Old Testament and in Judaism there was a strong sense of social responsibility. The collectors would go round every Friday morning and take a collection for the needy both in cash and in kind. Later the same day this would be distributed according to need. The fund from which this whole distribution was taken was known as the *Kuppah* or Basket.

This tradition clearly continued in the early church in Jerusalem, and a thoroughly estimable practice it was. However, the devil had taken this good practice and turned even this to his own ends — distraction and division.

EXPLANATION

Clearly the widows of the Greek-speaking Jewish Christians felt neglected; and probably they were. Only grace can break through the natural barriers of race, language and geography. Our natural selves soon build up the ramparts and rush to shelter behind them with our kith and kin. 'Stick to your own kind; one of your own kind' (West Side Story).

But then there is the more subtle tool in the hands of the devil: distraction. No one could say that the apostles were idle and clearly they were trying to do the loving thing as more and more of their time and energies were directed towards a social ministry. The care of the poor, underprivileged and widows was becoming a full-time programme. Two things were being neglected — preaching and prayer. So something had to be done if they were not to drift slowly further and further into a purely social gospel.

All Christians are called by their baptism into ministry. Yet there are varieties of gifts and ministries empowered and driven by the same, one Holy Spirit (1 Corinthians 12). Pastoral ministry (preaching and prayer) is not superior to social ministry and outreach. Different people are called to different ministries — and full-time ministries at that.

We can learn two lessons — one for the clergy and one for all baptised Christians — from this passage. The clergy neglect the priority of preaching and prayer at their peril. They need to give time for study, sermon-preparation and prayer at all times, upholding those whom they seek to minister to, in intercession, in counselling and in teaching. Thus the body is built up. That is a full-time job and must not be neglected for administration, which is also a ministry, neither inferior nor superior to the preaching ministry. (Paul lists administration in his list of gifts in 1 Corinthians 12:28). The clergy must stop trying to be jack-of-all trades and frankly resist the temptation to be seduced (sometimes only too willingly) into ministries that are apparently more obviously relevant and even sometimes more subtly rewarding — at least in the short run.

But there is the twist in the tale of this passage. Stephen and the seven, having been 'selected to concentrate on tables', end up in the firing line and Stephen is the first Christian martyr who dies for his 'sermon', his witness and his testimony. There is a kind of irony in this, but also a lesson.

All Christians are called to witness and testify, not just the 'professionals', to teach, preach and pray, Furthermore, 'tables and testimony' belong together, because all Christians (whatever their specific ministry) are called by baptism to witness and testify to the love of God made known to them in baptism. And notice further that 'lay' testimony and witness are often more effective, and powerful, and get under the skin more easily, than testimony and witness from those 'who are paid to do it'. Lay witness, at times and in places where you do not expect it, is especially effective and leads to confrontation and challenge far more than the formal testimony from the pulpit, where there is a captive audience.

So it is never the priority of the pure gospel over the social gospel; they belong together. However, those called to tables and social ministry can never get off the hook of witnessing and testifying to that love which motivates their ministry from start to finish. On the contrary, they, like Stephen, are the first in the firing line.

Ministering To The Ministry

But the Lord said to Ananias, 'Go! This man is my chosen instrument to carry my name before the Gentiles and their kings and before the people of Israel. I will show him how much he must suffer for my name.'

Then Ananias went to the house and entered it. Placing his hands on Saul, he said, 'Brother Saul, the Lord — Jesus, who appeared to you on the road as you were coming here — has sent me so that you may see again and be filled with the Holy Spirit.' Immediately, something like scales fell from Saul's eyes, and he could see again. He got up and was baptised, and after taking some food, he regained his strength.

Acts 9:15—19

EVENT

'Beyond doubt', says William Barclay, 'Ananias is one of the forgotten heroes of the Christian church.' Yes indeed, for Ananias was the first Christian to welcome Paul in the Christian community. Ananias took an enormous risk into going to Straight Street. (A precise address which still exists today: Straight Street runs from east to west and is the main street in the city of Damascus.) Ananias had wrestled and resisted in prayer and did not go very willingly — but he went. He was literally taking his life in his hands as he went into that house. He entered the room where Paul was praying and fasting — but this time not like the Pharisee in the temple, with eyes raised to heaven in self-righteousness, but with eyes cast down, still blind, seeking another kind of righteousness: the righteousness of God by which Paul, though a sinner, was reckoned righteous. It was that higher reality which had finally slain Paul in the spirit and brought him to his knees.

And then those opening words of Ananias: 'Brother Saul.' Saul could not see, but those words rang in his ears with gospel decibels: Saul a brother? But of course, since both Ananias and Saul were sons of the same God and Father of Jesus. There and then Saul laid hold of his baptismal rights: 'Ransomed, healed, restored, forgiven.'

EXPLANATION

The church is the expression of the gospel in flesh and blood terms. It is the true *philadelphia* — the community in which we experience the love of the Father mediated through the 'love of the brotherhood'. Saul had been forgiven vertically in his conversion on the Damascus road. He now had to have this endorsed horizontally, so that sin which was forgiven in heaven would indeed be seen and recognized to be forgiven on earth. The church is the forgiving, forgiven community.

So often the church fails to endorse the forgiveness of a wayward priest who has got into some kind of trouble. Is the church visible to the world's self-righteousness as the place where forgiveness is endorsed, expressed and lived out? For we need to be ministered to before we can minister. Peter was willing to wash people's feet; he resisted having his own feet washed. We need to be blessed, before we can bless; we need to be ministered to, before we can minister; and we need to be forgiven and to know we are loved, before we can forgive and go out of our way to love others. 'This is love,' says St

John, 'not that we loved God, but that he loved us and sent his Son . . . (1 John 4:10).

So often the clergy are the last to be ministered to; partly by their own professional fears and partly through a wrong deference that is paid to them. Priests visiting their bishop in hospital seldom ask to pray with him and to bless him. 'For you I am a bishop,' Augustine used to say, 'but among you I am a Christian.' Ananias was in the presence of the greatest missionary and apostle that the world has ever seen, but more fundamentally he had come into the presence of a new-born Christian, blind, confused and afraid. He ministered the gospel that day to Paul in all its fullness and he loved him with the love of Christ.

EXPERIENCE

Is the church today the sort of church which takes pastoral risks on all fronts? Is it too afraid of scandal and of what the world will say if forgiven sinners are allowed full communion? Do we live by grace and grace alone, believing in its all-sufficiency?

Then what about the clergy? Are they willing to be gospelled and ministered to, not only by fellow clergy but also by lay people, who often have wonderful ministries of healing, intercession and reassurance? Is the church evidently the expression of the gospel of forgiveness, living out its full implications — the community in which no stones are cast, because no one is without sin and undeserved forgiveness? That is what the world needs to see and know as it looks from the outside into the church.

A negro girl stood up after an evangelistic campaign conducted by Brian Green in America, to witness to what the mission had done for her. 'Through this campaign I have found Christ and he made me able to forgive the man who murdered my father.' Jesus made Ananias able to forgive Saul, one of the bitterest enemies of the Christian church. What Jesus did for Ananias and for that young negro girl he longs to do for his whole church and through the church for the whole world. But it starts and grows on a one-to-one basis: here and now, right where I am today. Forgiveness is not an idea, it is an event and it has, as it had for Paul, an address: first somewhere — like Calvary Hill — and then everywhere — like Straight Street — and then to the ends of the earth.

Truth and Love

Then the apostles and elders, with the whole church, decided to choose some of their own men and send them to Antioch with Paul and Barnabas. They choose Judas (called Barsabbas) and Silas, two men who were leaders among the brothers. With them they sent the following letter:

The apostles and elders, your brothers,

To the Gentile believers in Antioch, Syria and Cilicia:

Greetings.

We have heard that some went out from us without our authorisation and disturbed you, troubling your minds by what they said. So we all agreed to choose some men and send them to you with our dear friends Barnabas and Paul — men who have risked their lives for the name of our Lord Jesus Christ. Therefore we are sending Judas and Silas to confirm by word of mouth what we are writing. It seemed good to the Holy Spirit and to us not to burden you with anything beyond the following requirements: You are to abstain from food sacrificed to idols, from blood, from the meat of strangled animals and from sexual immorality. You will do well to avoid these things.

Farewell.

Acts 15:22—29

EVENT

A believing church will be a pastoral church, which clearly cares when the faithful are 'disturbed' (verse 24) with anything less than the truth of the full gospel.

Notice the remarkable wording to the letter which was to be personally delivered to the Gentile congregations. 'The apostles and elders, your brothers.' As a matter of fact the NIV translation misses the emphatic wording in the next sentence which should go on to read, 'To the Gentile brothers in Antioch, Syria and Cilicia.' This is a letter then between brothers and sisters. There is nothing paternalistic or condescending about this kind of pastoral ministry.

Proper care for the Gentile mission demanded that the church should exercise a consistent pastoral policy in keeping with the gospel and under the guidance of the Holy Spirit.

Here was a church and a leadership in that church which was ready to make decisions, and give leadership, fired by true pastoral concern. But all are under one father, because all see the real spiritual director of the church as the Holy Spirit who will lead the church into the fullness of catholic truth.

EXPLANATION

A dogmatic church needs to be tempered with the concerns of a pastoral church and at the same time a caring church must also care for the truth. Paul speaks of 'speaking the truth in love' (Ephesians 4:15). How hard it is to do just that.

Truth for the Christian is not an abstract dogma, rather it belongs within a relationship with the One who is himself the truth, but also the way and the life. The Christian church does not exist to draw up rules for right living or to be the moral police force of the secular world. Rather, the church is intended to bring people into communion with the One who is the truth. Then the disciple will live the life and walk in the way which reveals the truth. There is no place for the armchair theologian in Christianity. The theologian is the one who prays, lives and walks in the light of the truth. 'Theology,' says Anthony Bloom, 'is not knowing about God, even less what other people have written about God. Theology is knowing God.' The theologian necessarily wears stout walking shoes, with his feet set firmly on the way which leads to eternal life.

EXPERIENCE

The truth of the faith is communicated in this story of the first encyclical not just in the written word, but also personally in the hands of senior and responsible pastors who 'have risked their lives' for the sake of the truth which they proclaim. That is their principal qualification as truth-bearers — they have put their lives on every line of that letter!

Authority — that bedevilled word of the 'nineties' — is in direct relationship to obedience. Jesus spoke with authority (unlike the scribes and Pharisees) because he was himself a man under authority and the centurion (a man from within an authority structure) could spot it immediately. So with Mary — 'Do whatever he tells you' — and she should know, because she was conspiciously the first obedient human being to say an unqualified 'yes' to God.

Our church does indeed need to speak with new authority today, but its leadership must first be seen to live under authority (the authority of scripture, tradition and reason). That leadership must be seen to care about truth: the catholic church must at the same time be both compassionate and critical. Then they must care with a true passion for souls. So that the truth will be ministered with love and we will not lay upon people burdens too heavy to bear, while at the same time not raising a finger to help them to bear it (Luke 11:46).

Yes, the church individually and corporately needs spiritual direction and therefore spiritual directors, but this gospel must be ministered by shepherds who 'have risked their lives' for the sheep and who clearly live under the authority of the Holy Spirit. Then an authoritative church will be both a thinking church, a caring church and inevitably an evangelistic church — caring, compassionate and critical. 'Just look how these Christians care for each other!'

Pentecost Vigil Service

Preparing the Setting

The lighting in the church building is dimmed. The main doors should be closed, and where possible locked, before the service begins. The congregation have entered through other doors not usually used — e.g. an external west door to the vestry.

The choir and clergy have taken their places informally.

Each is given a candle as they enter the church.

The only candle in the church that is burning is the Paschal Candle.

Order of Service

INTRODUCTORY SENTENCE
When the day of Pentecost had fully come
they were all together in one place.

HYMN
Come, Holy Ghost, our souls inspire
or
Come, thou Holy Spirit, come
or
Come, thou Holy Paraclete

LITURGY OF THE SCRIPTURES
1st Reading : Genesis 1:1—10
Psalm : 33:1—11
2nd Reading : 1 Kings 18:30—39
Psalm : 36:5—10
3rd Reading : Isaiah 6:1—8
Psalm : 104:25—37
4th Reading : Ezekiel 37:1—14
Psalm : 145
New Testament Reading : Acts 2:1—21

GRADUAL HYMN
O thou who camest from above

(During the singing of this hymn all the candles in the church are lit to solemnly honour the gospel reading of the words of our Lord.)

Gospel : John 20:19—23

THE HOMILY
(At the end of the Gospel all extinguish their candles.)

BAPTISM & CONFIRMATION
(Where possible Baptism & Confirmation now follow.)

HYMN
Holy Spirit, ever dwelling (NEH 141)
(During the singing of this hymn the people's candles are re-lit in readiness for the Renewal of Baptismal Vows.)

RENEWAL OF BAPTISMAL VOWS
After Renewal of Baptismal Vows all kneel and sing:

Spirit of the Living God
and/or
Breathe on me, breath of God

LAYING ON OF HANDS & ANOINTING
(During the singing of the hymns the Bishop or Priest administers the Laying on of Hands and Anointing.)

CONCLUDING RITE
The Deacon takes a large copy of the Holy Scriptures from the Altar and hands it to the Bishop, if present, or his deputy, the Parish Priest.

THE SOLEMN PROCESSION OF THE SCRIPTURES
Just as the presence of Christ is reverenced in the Sacrament of the Eucharist, so we reverence the presence of God in the Sacrament of the Word. Thus, the Scriptures are now honoured with all the splendour we can muster in a solemn procession round the nave of the church.

We have a gospel to proclaim

The procession eventually comes to rest at the main doors of the church. The Deacon, or other minister, then proclaims in a loud voice:

Go into all the world and preach
the gospel to the whole creation.

The main doors of the church are now flung open. The candles of the people are exchanged for lighted torches as they leave the church following behind the Bishop/Priest holding high the Scriptures. The procession continues round the outside of the church building and then on to a natural meeting place within the parish or district (e.g. Shopping Centre/ Town Hall/School).

The assembly gathers round the Scriptures and the Deacon reads the Gospel.

The Gospel : John 1:1—14a

A copy of the New Testament or one of the Gospels is distributed to everyone present.

After the Dismissal each takes their copy of the New Testament or Gospel and lighted torch and visits the home of a neighbour or friend and hands on to them the Testament/Gospel and the lighted torch — a living act and symbol of the Pentecost event.

For background and general advice, see Michael Marshall, *Renewal in Worship* (Marshalls 1982), especially chapter 6, 'Signs, symbols and ceremonies'.